DATE DUE			

The American Journalists

HEARST AND HIS ENEMIES

Edward T. O'Loughlin

ARNO
&
The New York Times

Collection Created and Selected
by Charles Gregg of Gregg Press

Publisher's Note:

This edition has been reprinted from the best
available copy. All technical resources have
been utilized to reproduce illustrations with
greatest clarity, but, in some cases, without
success. The total content of the book is of
such value that we beg the indulgence of our
readers for these small imperfections.

Reprint edition 1970 by Arno Press Inc.

LC# 76-125710
ISBN 0-405-01691-3

The American Journalists
ISBN for complete set: 0-405-01650-6

Reprinted from a copy in
The New York Historical Society Library

Manufactured in the United States of America

HEARST

AND HIS

ENEMIES

Compiled for

THE COMMITTEE OF RELATIVES OF
AMERICAN SOLDIERS, SAILORS AND MARINES
═══ OF GREATER NEW YORK ═══

By

EDWARD T. O'LOUGHLIN
Three times Register of Kings County, N. Y.

48 PAGES   30 ILLUSTRATIONS

PRICE TEN CENTS

Tumulty Sends President's Thanks

© CLINEDINST. WASH. D.C.
JOSEPH P. TUMULTY
Secretary to the President, who sent the
letter of thanks in the name of Woodrow
Wilson.

A MONG the letters, thanking the **Hearst pa**pers for their work in the war, **is one from** the White House, forwarded by **Joseph P.** Tumulty, on April 5, 1918, to W. **P. Anderson,** circulation manager of the New York *American.* It reads as follows:

" THE WHITE HOUSE

" Washington

" **April 5, 1918.**

" My **dear Mr. Anderson:**

" **The President has asked me to** thank you **cordially for your** letter of April 4th, with e**nclosures, which he has noted** with a great **deal of interest.** He **genuinely** appreciates your co-operation **and support.**

"Sincerely yours,

" J. P. TUMULTY,

" Secretary to the **President."**

"A Genuine Service" Says McAdoo

"YOU are rendering a genuine service to the country " is the way William G. **McAdoo,** Secretary of the Treasury, expressed it, in a letter which he sent to Mr. Roy D. **Keehn,** manager of the Hearst Chicago papers, **in speaking of the aid given to the Liberty Loan drive.**

Secretary McAdoo, in writing to Mr. Keehn, under date of September 1, 1917, said:

" Many thanks for the fine support the Examiner is giving the Liberty Loan **and** for its generous treatment of me. **You are rendering a genuine service to the** country, and I want you to know how deeply I appreciate it. Warm reg**ards,**

" W. G. McA**doo."**

SECRETARY OF WAR THANKS HEARST PAPERS

SECRETARY OF WAR BAKER, on April 29, 1918, wrote a letter to W. P. Anderson of the *New York American*, in which he said the campaign conducted by the Hearst papers was "essentially helpful" in war work. He said:

"**This sort of editorial seems to me essentially helpful,** because it has a lot of reliable information and tends to show in an effective way the progress which the country is making in many of the vital factors connected with the war."

High Praise from the Head of the Navy

THOSE who hear Hearst's foes denounce him should read this letter from no less a personage than Josephus Daniels, Secretary of the Navy. It was sent April 1, 1917, when Hearst was working with might and main to aid in every way the preparations for war. It follows:

Here is Mr. Daniels, head of the Navy, smiling at the absurdity of the stories told about Hearst. Read his letter and see what HE thinks.

"EDITOR *New York American:*

"**The page in the Hearst newspapers today devoted to a campaign in aid of recruiting shows a splendid spirit of patriotism.** You have made known clearly to the public the need in the navy of young men of spirit and ambition to serve their country in an emergency.

"Such work is manifestly a great public service. It is particularly a great service because done at a time when the enlisted personnel is of the highest grade and when it is desirable that more of such men should be added as soon as possible to the ranks of a navy which in respect of personnel is the best in the world.

"**The plan indicated on the recruiting page of the *New York American* today will be followed undoubtedly by very material and gratifying results.** Certainly it sets forth advantages which have never before been offered to the men of any navy in the world.

"I assume that the same practical interest as that shown by the *New York American* is being taken in the recruiting by all of the Hearst papers. Work in such cities as San Francisco, Los Angeles and Chicago, similar to that being done in New York, will undoubtedly result in a notable increase in the enlisted force, and that very promptly.

"We hope to have 25,000 more at least very soon. **The efforts of the *New York American* will contribute very largely in carrying out the purposes of the navy at this time.**

"With kind regards, believe me

"Sincerely yours,
"JOSEPHUS DANIELS."

THAT DOESN'T LOOK AS IF HEARST WAS IMPEDING THE WAR, DOES IT?

A Million Circulation !
Most Popular Publication in the Navy !

Facts and Figures!
Facsimiles!

Becker's Bolo Pasha
Charges and Prison
Record of Confessed
Criminals he
Used in Attempted
"Frame-up"

The "Tribune"
and its Owner
Related to English
Nobility and
Heavily Interested in
New York Central
and Allied Lines
which
Hearst Brought to the
Bar of Justice

The Mills Estate
Fed by the Watered
Stock of a Score
of Big Railroads

The Details of a Plot
that will Amaze You!

Propaganda of
Misquotation and
Misrepresentation

Lies About the
Lusitania!

THE friends of William Randolph Hearst listened, for a long time, to the lies scattered broadcast, by his foes —the paid and organized agents of predatory plutocracy.

His enemies said he was opposed to the war; his spoken word and editorial expression, as well as the news columns of his papers, refuted this, on every page, on every day.

The National Security League viciously attacked his Americanism; we found this organization backed by all the profiteers in the big war whose dealings Hearst had exposed.

The Tribune was the vicious mouthpiece of the attack; we found its owner deeply interested in railroad concerns which tried to rob the city and which robbery Hearst halted.

His enemies tried to link Hearst's name with that of Bolo Pasha; we find that Bolo really came to America to get extensive credit from the banking house of Morgan & Co., friend of the profiteers. Why was this fact hidden from the public for seventeen months?

They said Hearst condoned the sinking of the Lusitania; as a matter of fact, he called it " wholesale, wanton murder."

Becker's defamations against Hearst were spread far and wide; we found, in the evidence, that Becker's whole case rested upon the word of a confirmed criminal on parole from the Tombs, who had admitted his part in an $800,000 swindle!

COMMITTEE OF RELATIVES OF MEN WHO SERVED THE COLORS.

Excerpts from
Evidence!
Testimonials!

Cartoons that Tell
Stories and Give the
Lie to Calumnies!

The $1,000,000
"Slush" Fund of the
National Security
League—the Big
Profiteering Concerns
Behind this
Un-American Body!

The Letters which
Bolo Pasha bore
to J. P. Morgan and
Hidden Documents!

The Blood-Stained
Profits Made in
the Big War

A Hundred
Amazing Features
About the Campaign
of Calumny
Launched to Destroy
the Name of an
American Champion
of the American
People!

A Handbook for Real Americans, who may Use it to Show the Real
Facts Behind the Calumnies Spread by Organized
Trust Agents!

THE REAL TRUTH ABOUT HEARST'S BIG WORK IN WINNING THE WAR!

4

The Truth About the Trust Plot
Behind the Attack on Hearst

EDWARD T. O'LOUGHLIN

The compiler of this pamphlet, who was elected three times, by the people of Brooklyn, as Registrar of Kings County. He has known Hearst intimately for fifteen years, and says: "There is not a more loyal American in the country today than William Randolph Hearst. I, who have blood kin, enlisted with the colors, am proud of him, his words and deeds. He is the victim of the most atrocious plot ever concocted by the minions of corrupt wealth. We shall all live to see his traducers condemned and Hearst himself triumphantly vindicated."

FAIR-MINDED men and women, who have been studying, impartially, the various phases of the campaign now being waged mercilessly and, to a great extent, maliciously, by certain interests, including some so-called patriotic organizations, against William Randolph Hearst, are gradually, but none the less surely and convincedly, coming to the conclusion that the fight is not an honest one—that there is something more behind this unparalleled assault than appears on the surface and that it is too brazenly one sided, in its capitalistic coloring, to be what the language of the street calls " on the level."

A cold, impartial study of the facts is necessary before one can form a just conclusion, and we are sure that the great mass of Americans, who believe in fair play, will soon come to view this question in its proper light, and when once the motive behind the attack on Hearst is understood, there will be revealed one of the most gigantic plots ever launched to destroy an individual citizen.

And yet the fight against Hearst is not directed so much against the individual as against the principles for which he stands and which he has enunciated and propounded for years past. The patriotism alleged by his defamers is seen to be but camouflage, designed to mask the ulterior purposes which they have in view. His defamers, in large part, are found to be led on by clever, shrewd and ruthless agents for various conscienceless corporations which Hearst, in the past, has vigorously and courageously assailed as enemies of the people. These have seized upon solitary statements, taken from the body of inspiringly patriotic editorials, and served them up to the public in such distorted shape as to give a totally different meaning from that which the statement, in its entirety, originally conveyed.

The campaign of calumny stands out as a naked conspiracy engineered by those who, in the past, have been exposed in the act of exploiting the public and who have a long-standing grudge to settle with the man who exposed them.

PUBLIC WITH HEARST

These agents of criminal wealth have succeeded, by using the well-known channels of trust agencies and the subsidized press, which depends for its existence upon corporate favor, in creating, in certain restricted

MENACE OF BIG MONEY

What Hearst Says of the Foundation Fund to Finance Plutocracy

"**T**HE enormous amounts of money which the predatory rich have accumulated are used to maintain the unequal conditions under which predatory wealth prospers, and under which it tyrannically rules and robs the public.

"An estimate by a leading financier * * * places the income of the Rockefeller fortune at twelve million dollars a month. Such immense wealth is a great and genuine menace to the republican institutions of this country.

" The conditions which permit the accumulation of such wealth are undemocratic, and will, if continued, eventually involve the republic in ruin."

circles, an abnormally unjust estimate of the man who has done so much to protect the people and to hinder corporate greed. The propaganda, however, overreached itself. It brought a violent reaction, for there are thousands among the thinking element who saw through this disguised attack and rallied to the standard of Hearst. This is shown in the fact that since this campaign against Hearst began, the circulation of his newspapers has risen to figures never believed to be attainable by a daily newspaper.

At the very height of the campaign against him, and while an organized band were engaged in advising the public not to read his newspapers, the circulation of the American rose to over a million copies on Sunday alone. This was the answer of the thinking class to the charge made by the Wall Street agents and the societies which they controlled.

MILLION DOLLAR "SLUSH" FUND

A fair sample of these subsidized organizations, controlled by capital, is the National Security League, which is even now before Congress undergoing investigation. It was revealed that **a huge " slush " fund had been used to attack the political character of nearly 300 members of Congress.** One of its agents admitted that the society handled over $1,000,000. Among the contributors of large sums were the Carnegie Foundation, which gave $150,000, and the Rockefeller Foundation, which sent $50,000, to be used by this character destroying organization.

Hearst has been one of the bitterest foes of The Standard Oil Trust. It was he who exposed the secret control which Standard Oil enjoyed over the national government, when he revealed photographic copies of letters sent by the Vice-President of the Oil Trust to various senators, instructing them how to vote and kill certain measures intended for the public benefit, and enclosing checks for $25,000 each to senators.

These were the famous Archbold letters, beginning " My Dear Senator," and which Mr. Hearst read in the presidential campaign of 1908, creating a sensation which set the whole country rocking with indignation. These letters, beginning " My Dear Senator," usually ended with the following: " Enclosed you will find certificate for $25,000 which I have placed to your credit."

Everyone remembers how the Hearst papers assailed the Foundation influence in city government, during the Municipal campaign of 1917, and how Hearst exposed the

---

Warning From An Insider!

"LET us not for one moment think that this great war can stop without a reaction of some kind, and one equal in magnitude to the initial action. The law of equal and opposite reaction still rules the world. Russia, the most autocratic nation, swung furthest to hideous socialism. Germany blew up next, simply because her masses were so completely suppressed. THE PEOPLE OF AMERICA HAVE NOT ·YET REVOLTED BECAUSE THEY HAVE NOT YET BEEN SUPPRESSED. America has been under the wise leadership of men who understand. But no men—however wise—can now prevent some great change from following this war. The question is: Shall we all voluntarily give up something, or shall we all run the risk of losing everything? "
—From the Babson forecast of financial events, issued to his clients, among merchants, bankers and investors, under date of November 19, 1918.

HOW HEARST HELPED THE RED CROSS

HIS newspapers furnished free their best cartoonists and writers from the *New York American* and the *Evening Journal* staff to the Red Cross Committee and published, from May 18 to May 27 (the week of the first Red Cross Drive), 204¾ columns promoting its success.

secret hold which the Rockefeller and other foundations sought to gain over the school and charities systems of the City of New York.

THE DISGUISE OF PATRIOTISM

The venom of the Foundation hatred, and the attempted revenge for this attack by the Hearst newspapers, is revealed in the fight which the National Security League, supported by corporate interests, is now waging against Hearst, under the disguise of patriotism.

In all the campaign of calumny, carried on against Hearst, by such societies as the Standard Oil controlled National Security League, not one word of praise is given for the great work which the Hearst papers performed during the war—for the campaign, in which they led, for the draft bill through which Uncle Sam raised his armies; to raise money for all the Liberty loans; for the Red Cross, Y. M. C. A., Salvation Army, Knights of Columbus, Jewish Welfare Board, the War Saving Stamps drives, and every other great movement to make the war a success.

From the moment the President of the United States threw down the gauntlet of battle in the face of the Prussian Autocrat, and even long before this, Hearst and his newspapers lined themselves up in the foremost ranks of the despots' most vehement foes. No one can read the Hearst newspapers, as they were published during that soul-stirring time, without coming to the most emphatic and satisfied conclusion that they, of all the papers published in the United States, were the most clamorous and insistent that the country should be fully prepared in every way to meet the issue of war.

Looking back, in a cold-blooded, conscientious, and impartial way over the bound files of the New York American and the Evening Journal, and studying the contents seriously, one is convinced that only the most malicious could pretend to find anything except the most warm-blooded support of the government.

The trust criminals who had felt the sting of Hearst's editorial lash; who hated Hearst with a hate that was mortal; who had been "laying to get even," as it were, for years, thought they saw, in the exciting period of war hysteria, an opportunity that was too golden to miss, and they began the campaign of misrepresentation, villification and denunciation that was to sweep him and all his beliefs, as they imagined, to destruction.

> T HE Hearst papers collected and forwarded to Congress **two million and eighty thousand** individual petitions, asking Congress to pass the selective draft law promptly. And Congress passed it.
>
> AND YET THE ENEMIES OF HEARST SAY HE IMPEDED THE WAR.

Were it not for the fact that his newspapers were so widely read, and so many millions knew the truth about the splendid patriotic work being done by his newspapers—the work they did before and during the war, the tremendous amount of space they devoted to all the movements to speed up the work of the war—this monstrous campaign might have succeeded.

It was cunningly masked behind the mantle of patriotic purpose; it was directed by organizations, the inside workings of which the people had no means of viewing, and, in the beginning, the master minds of finance, who pulled all the wires and set the wheels in motion, were so far in the background that the real purpose of the assault was not then divined by the general public.

HOW THE FACTS CAME TO LIGHT

It was only when those who knew the sources of this campaign of villification began to make careful investigations that the facts gradually came to the surface. THE INJUSTICE OF THE WHOLE THING STOOD OUT.

In the series of infamous pamphlets that were issued and mailed broadcast to every patriotic society in the country, there is not one word of the work done by Hearst to help

(*Continued on page* 8.)

The Lie about the Lusitania!

"T HE sinking of the Lusitania with her heavy freightage of peaceful travelers, including hundreds of women and children, is not an act of war: IT IS A DEED OF WHOLESALE MURDER."

This is what the Hearst papers said on May 8, 1915, the morning after the tragedy— and with all the emphasis of capital letters.

And yet the enemies of Hearst have brazenly said he "condoned the sinking of the Lusitania."

the passage of the selective draft law; his private help to promote the various drives to secure volunteer enlistments, and the aid given to every movement to assist men in all branches of the service, as well as those who were serving the army and navy, here and abroad, in works of mercy.

THANKS FROM WILSON DOWN

Almost criminal is the brazen silence of these organized defamers concerning the fact that every big official in the country from the President of the United States down has thanked Hearst and his newspapers for the aid they rendered in winning the war. Mountains of testimonials from all sources are piled on the desks of Hearst and his editors, thanking them for the part they played in helping every drive.

These letters, unsolicited, and genuine, and enthusiastic, come from the heads of the army, the navy, the managing directors of Red Cross, Y. M. C. A., Knights of Columbus, Salvation Army, Liberty Loan, Jewish Welfare and other drives.

THEY CONTAIN, AMONG OTHERS, TESTIMONIALS FROM WOODROW WIL-SON, VICE-PRESIDENT MARSHALL, SECRETARY OF WAR BAKER, SECRETARY OF THE NAVY DANIELS, DIRECTOR GENERAL OF THE UNITED STATES SHIP-PING BOARD, SCHWAB, AND WILLIAM G. McADOO, FOR THE SUPPORT GIVEN BY THE HEARST PAPERS IN EVERY AVENUE OF INFLUENCE TO MAKE THE WAR A SUCCESS.

HEARST'S WARNING ABOUT SLAVERY!

"FOR of what use, citizens, of what use have been all the nation's sacrifices in war abroad, if the result is to be slavery at home—if those who stand up bravely for the freedom of the press, the freedom of opinion, the freedom of speech, the freedom of assemblage, are to be hounded, defamed, persecuted and menaced in person and property and reputation by spies, agents and tools of official bureaucrats and hidden predatory interests?"

—From an editorial in the Hearst newspapers, a few days after Becker's Bolo Pasha story had been exploded before the Senate investigating committee.

The capitalistically controlled character assassins who are attacking Hearst have spread false stories about the attitude of men in the service. Those of us, who have relatives in the army and navy, have personally questioned our own relatives and other men returning from service, and find that Hearst is the idol of the men.

MARINES ORDER 20,000 COPIES

The Hearst papers are read with enthusiasm by the men in all branches of the service. One letter which the Hearst organization prizes is written by the Major General Commandant of the Marines, asking for 20,000 copies of the *American* and *Journal*, containing an editorial on the valor of the marines, which the Commandant desired the men in the Corps to read. The Commander of the Great Lakes Training Station sent a letter to the Chicago Hearst papers, which was lavish in its praise of the work done by the Hearst organization in that part of the country.

Out of Hearst's great printing plants, throughout the country, hundreds of men have gone into the service, to answer the call to arms. In addition to those who have entered the service, there are others, who have sons, brothers, nephews or cousins, who have donned the uniform of both army and navy. These men feel keenly the malicious libel upon the head of their industrial organization. Many of them are weary of the one-sided campaign of vilification and mis-representation, and desire to see the facts set forth so that honest-minded men and women may form their just opinions of the character of those who waged this cowardly capitalistic war on Hearst.

LIP-PATRIOTS LEAD THE ATTACK

Many of those loudest in the campaign of vilification against Hearst have no real connection with the war whatever. These lip-patriots, living upon the fat of profiteering enterprises, which Hearst has, time and again, flayed in his editorial columns, and which waxed fat and rich at the expense of the men who went across the seas, were careful to remain at home, while men of the Hearst service answered the call to the colors.

E LIHU ROOT, who is one of the highly paid corporation attorneys, vehment in his vilification of Hearst, is said to have hid under a bed, during the Civil War, when the recruiting sergeant came his way to seek volunteers. This may or may not be a playful exaggeration of what has really a basis in fact. It is not on record, however, that Root, although of fighting age at the time of that great conflict, offered himself for the salvation of the Union.

When we find these assailants of Hearst deliberately concealing great truths about Hearst's work for the successful winning of the war, we are forced to the conclusion that the fight against him is not only not sincere—but is desperately false, inaugurated, if you will, to create an impression, in the popular mind, which if successfully created, may destroy his effectiveness as an agent for popular good.

When we find him, alone, made the target for the assaults of such corporation agents, and their closely controlled bodies, it begins to look, to us, as if the object of the assault is more personal than patriotic.

When we find these assailants, practically all birds of a feather, flocking together under the wing of Wall Street protection, we begin to see that it is Hearst, the radical; Hearst the foe of criminal wealth, the friend of the working class, and the defender of the peoples rights, that is being assailed.

A glance at the editorial pages of the Hearst newspapers, any day, will show why great corporation criminals and their wily, high-paid attorneys, hate Hearst. The stinging satire of the daily Brisbane column, the lashing force of effective cartoons and the black-typed exposes of the exploiters, in all avenues of trust domination, explain the undying animosity of these organized villifiers of Hearst.

WHY THEY REALLY HATE HEARST

It is the terrific sledge-hammer truths contained in editorial opinions that daily display the wrongs of the people, that call malefactors of great wealth to account, that pillory profiteers, among whom are many of the "patrioteers" now assailing him; that warn the criminal rich not to imitate—the brainless Bourbons, who brought on the French Revolution—these are the things which his enemies really detest and would like to destroy in destroying Hearst.

If criminal wealth, under the false guise of patriotism, is permitted ruthlessly to defame Hearst, what hope is there for any individual or group of individuals, who may incur the anger of this dangerous class, and who may not have, to support them, the powerful weapon of publicity which is the mainstay of Hearst against all such attacks?

The criminally rich instigators of this attack upon Hearst may find that they have started something which they cannot finish. No man can tell just where this fight will spread, what course it may take, how far it may go, or where it will end. The ugly facts, regarding the $1,000,000 "slush" fund of the National Security League, contributed largely through agents of the great profiteering trusts, and which organization took a prominent part in the campaign against Hearst, have only recently opened the eyes of the public to the financial character of the society which pretended to be interested solely in the prosecution of our late war.

LED BY BIG PROFITEERS

Some of these contributors to the fund are known to represent great corporations, which have profited enormously as a result of the war. This is not a wholesome fact to display, in large letters, before the eyes of the masses who have suffered all sorts of privations to make this war against autocracy a success. Our soldiers and sailors, who fought on land and sea to preserve our liberties against the encroachment of despotic militarism, yielded their services and were willing to give up their lives, if need be, for the stipulated compensation of $30 a month. Small business men patriotically acquiesced to a loss of all their profits as a result of the conditions brought on by the war.

And now it appears, as the light of publicity is let in, through the channels of the very investigation which they themselves instigated, that the men and the agencies most instrumental in the campaign against Hearst are those whose profiteering concerns realized millions, aye billions, out of the blood of their fellowmen during the stressful, terrible period of the world-wrecking war.

The campaign against Hearst is thus disclosed as no longer an individual affair, but, apparently, an incident in something far graver. Hearst has been the journalistic bulwark between the masses and the predatory interests. The campaign is not aimed at him alone—but against the popular principles for which he stands. It is the first gun in the battle of a greedy, restricted, daring privileged class against the masses.

(Continued on page 10.)

WOUNDED HEROES OF WAR RESENT ATTACKS MADE UPON HEARST

MEMORIALS containing thousands upon thousands of signatures of soldiers, sailors and marines,—men wounded upon the battlefields of France, their relatives, and veterans of the Spanish-American and Civil Wars,—have been lodged with Mayor John F. Hylan, at the City Hall, in New York, praising him for appointing William Randolph Hearst, Chairman of the Committee to Welcome Returning Troops. These memorials express the thanks of the men and their relatives for the fight which Hearst is making to secure for " the boys " the six months extra pay to which they are entitled and which Hearst says is needed " to tide them over " until they can find employment, on their return to civil life.

These memorials give the lie to the stories spread by the agents of corporate wealth that the soldiers, sailors and marines are not with Hearst in the fight he is making to win for them, their well deserved rights.

These "captains of industry," attacking Hearst, are not keen for the "six months' pay" propaganda, because it means another assault upon their fat war-fed pocketbook!

Six Months' Pay for "The Boys" While They Look for a Job!

HEARST was the very first to come out boldly, and demand that the Government give the returning soldiers, sailors and marines six months' pay in advance, while they looked for a job, after demobilization. He urged the immediate honorable discharge instead of keeping the men cooped up in camps "to avoid a glut in the labor market."

"Words of gratitude, alone, are not sufficient," says Hearst. "If our people and our government are truly grateful to these heroic soldiers, then they should be treated with more consideration than is being shown.

"The Government took them almost without a moment's warning from their various occupations, trained them to be soldiers and sent them abroad to win the battles which they have gloriously won.

"Now these Americans are returning to their country, some to find their places still open to them, some to find their positions filled, some to find it necessary to hunt for weeks or months before they can again secure the steady and satisfactory employment from which they were taken to serve their native land.

"Is it not merely the most simple justice, the most meagre generosity, for the Government to pay these returned soldiers their military wages for a period of six months, until they can settle back into the daily occupation from which they were hurried to fight for their country and their country's cause?"

The Hearst papers, every day, since the armistice was signed, have printed a petition which the public is asked to sign, calling on the Secretary of War and the Secretary of the Navy to secure the authority necessary to pay the men, mustered out of service, their six months' pay in advance. Hundreds of thousands of signatures have been secured and forwarded to Washington. Legislatures have been urged to adopt resolutions and a bill has been introduced into Congress.

"This is not charity," says Hearst. "It is only common sense, and it should be done. We have millions and millions to send to Europe. Let us spend at least a few millions on the boys who did the fighting."

(Continued from page 9.)

It has got beyond their control. It is no longer Hearst's fight; but yours and mine. It is no longer Hearst who is attacked, but your liberties and mine.

If, however, we allow Hearst, the boldest, most courageous and powerful of our champions, to be downed, the battle will be so much the harder for the rest of us to fight.

Hearst Being Fought By Foes of Workingmen Says Head of State Labor Federation

(Q) JAMES P. HOLLAND

PRESIDENT JAMES P. HOLLAND of the New York State Federation of Labor, says the assault on Hearst means that "the industrial pirates" and "financial freebooters" are now "fighting with their backs to the wall." In this last stand of theirs, he declares, they are attempting "to discredit and destroy" those who have exposed them.

Mr. Holland wrote to Mr. Hearst on December 30, 1918.

This campaign, he says, is waged "**because those selfish and protected interests have been affected through the adoption of progressive legislation urged by organized labor and advocated by your newspapers.**

"Through your newspapers you have advocated a free press, free speech and war revenues to be derived from incomes, inheritance and excess profit taxes, the care of our soldiers and sailors, so that they would not have to worry about their future, the establishment of the widows' pension system, workmen's compensation, elimination of child labor, federal insurance for all the people, improvement of our educational standards, minimum wages for women and minors, government ownership of railroads, telegraph and telephone systems, federal control of coal mines, water power and other natural resources, the establishment of the eight-hour day and the Americanization of all foreigners, woman suffrage and many other matters of great benefit to humanity.

"Naturally the advocacy of these necessary and humane measures has aroused the bitter antagonism of those who profit by these inhuman conditions, and in order to prevent further enlightenment of the people along these lines, they attack the persons responsible for them."

A Race of "Satisfied Serfs"

PETER J. BRADY, President of the Allied Printing Trades Council of New York State, and Chairman of the Education Committee of the New York State Federation of Labor, pointed out, some time ago, the menace of the Rockefeller Foundation in its attempt to make "satisfied serfs" of the children in the public schools of New York City. It was the celebrated Gary plan. Brady quoted from a pamphlet issued by Frederick T. Gates, head of the Rockefeller General Education Board, who wrote as follows:

"In our dreams we have limitless resources, and **the people yield themselves with perfect docility to our moulding hand.** The present education conventions fade from our minds, and unhampered by tradition we work our own good will upon a grateful and responsive rural folk. We shall not try to make these people or any of their children into philosophers or men of learning or of science. We have not to raise up from among them authors, editors, poets or men of letters. We shall not search for embryo great artists, painters, musicians, nor will we cherish even the humbler ambition to raise up from among them lawyers, doctors, preachers, politicians, statesmen of whom we now have ample supply. **The task that we set before ourselves is a very simple as well as a very beautiful one, to train these people as we find them to a perfectly ideal life just where they are.**

"So we will organize our children into a little community and teach them to do in a perfect way THE THINGS THEIR FATHERS AND MOTHERS ARE DOING in an imperfect way, in the homes, in the shop and on the farm."

Here was a plan to raise a race of satisfied peasants who would work the will of Rockefeller. HEARST KILLED THIS!

How Propaganda Against Hearst was Spread by Lying Pamphlets and Agents of Profiteers!

The Million Dollar "Slush" Fund of the National Security League put up by Powder Kings, Railway Wreckers, Munitioneers and others who Reaped Billions of Profits out of a War that Cost 8,000,000 Lives!

© T. COLEMAN DUPONT

The "Powder King," whose firm is said to have grown fabulously rich out of the profits of the war. Hearst suggested that Uncle Sam should commandeer all munition plants for the period of the war. This would have hurt Mr. DuPont's pocket dreadfully.

A S we review the magnitude of the plot by which the agents of profiteering concerns sought to destroy the name of Hearst; the widespread propaganda of vilification and misrepresentation that was launched through the medium of lying pamphlets, containing distorted and mutilated excerpts of editorials; the organized movement to corrupt the membership of patriotic bodies, throughout the land, and the methods by which such membership was falsely led to believe the most villainous statements about Hearst, we are amazed, at this late day—when the whole disgusting and appalling truth is known—not so much at the fact that so many sincere and honest patriots were deluded, but that the instigators of this monstrous, moneyed conspiracy dared to go as far as they did, before their dastardly purpose was laid bare under the searching scrutiny of a Congressional investigation.

For it was only when Congress, smarting under the injustice of similar attacks, haled the officials of the National Security League before it and challenged this character-destroying organization to produce proof of its statements that the real nature of the assailants became known, **the sinister hand of profiteering wealth behind it became disclosed and the existence of a huge "slush" fund of more than $1,000,000, contributed largely by those who had grown fabulously rich through the horrors and agony of war, was exposed to the gaze of a wondering, indignant public.**

Then, for the first time, as the investigation began to tear aside the mask of patriotism that veiled the true purpose of the body, was the motive for its existence and its mission

---

Two Billions in War Profits

U NITED STATES Senator Hiram Johnson, speaking in Washington, recently, said that $2,000,000,000 OF WAR PROFITS HAD BEEN PERMITTED TO GO INTO THE COFFERS OF THOSE WHO COINED PROFITS OUT OF THE WAR, and this loss will have to be made up in the future by taxes on normal business.

—News item from a daily paper.

The Beneficiaries are those attacking Hearst!

made fully known. Then was told for the first time, unwillingly at first, but dragged, sentence by sentence, from the lips of the officers, the real truth about the purpose of the National Security League, the manner in which it was financed, the men of millions who financed it and the reasons of revenge which they had for attacking those who had in any way attempted to stand between them and further exploitation of the people.

It was when the existence of the $1,000,000 ".slush" fund came to light that the skeletons in the closet of predatory wealth began to rattle and all the shameful secrets came forth.

One by one the heavy tragedians in this sordid drama of corrupt wealth stalked forth across the stage and the public began to understand the reason for all the long, sustained and powerful assault made, not alone upon Hearst, but likewise upon the men in Congress who had dared to vote for measures taxing excess profits of the war, and for other measures that would have relieved the people, in large part, of the burden of war and placed the expense upon the shoulders of those who were reaping tremendous fortunes out of the circumstance of war!

PROFITEERS BEHIND THE LEAGUE

A S the list of contributors to this huge "slush" fund of $1,000,000 was dragged out into the light of day, there appeared the names of powder kings, great railway stock jobbers, manipulators of the money market, men whose names have been titles of terror in Wall Street for years, munitioneers and profiteers of every size and description whose ramifications of activity have entered every avenue where a tainted dollar was to be made by the blood and blistering breath of war.

Such a roll for such a fund and for such a society, supposedly organized for the patriotic purpose of protecting the people in time of war!

This was the "loyal" League that dared to brand men with the stigma of disloyalty!

While a million men crossed the sea and marched to the battlefields of the world's most awful war; while hundreds of thousands died that democracy might win; while the fathers and mothers and sisters and wives of these men starved and slaved at home, that the sacred cause might triumph, these men, hiding behind the mask of patriotism, safe in the security of concealment, but branding others as "disloyal," remained to fatten, like vultures upon the carcasses of the dead!

ⓒ S. STANWOOD MENKEN

S. Stanwood Menken, who once, in an unguarded moment, said something nice about Hearst, and the work done by his newspapers. Menken said: "William Randolph Hearst has been one of our greatest leaders for national security and universal training. When we were practically without any support he sprang to the front to carry on the cause. He has been there ever since. As in all things he takes up, he has done this with his whole heart and his full strength." He was practically kicked out of the presidency for having said this. The trust owners behind the League considered it too nice a thing to say about Hearst.

You can begin to understand, now, gentle reader, where all the money came from that financed all those silly but simultaneous attacks that were launched upon the Hearst newspapers some time ago. Did it ever occur to you how some of those cheap little "patrioteers" whom you met at railroad stations, asking you not to read the Hearst papers, could find so much loose time to do such work? You may rest assured that the loose change of the "loyal" Security League was working overtime.

You can understand, also, in a way, the impelling motive behind the grossly malicious attacks of the New York *Tribune,* which became the mouthpiece of this gang and which published lying, misleading pamphlets that were distributed to every patriotic society within a radius of a thousand miles.

It was one drunken, plutocratic orgy of misspent money while it lasted; but it put many a yard of the long green into many a needy pocket while it raged.

"THE Rockefeller Foundation is probably the most menacing influence in the public life of America. The sniveling hypocrisy that stands WITH A BIBLE IN ONE HAND AND A BRIBE IN THE OTHER has been thoroughly exposed heretofore in the articles of Ida Tarbell in McClure's Magazine and in the widely published Standard Oil Letters."

—WILLIAM RANDOLPH HEARST.

SPREAD OF LYING PAMPHLETS

These lying pamphlets which were spread broadcast, simultaneously with the attacks launched from the headquarters of the National Security League, were a feature of this campaign of calumny and misrepresentation. They consisted of "extracts" taken supposedly from editorials which had appeared in the Hearst newspapers before and during the war. They were prepared with infinite cunning and, in mutilated or otherwise distorted form, were audaciously put forth as authentic reproductions of editorial opinion. The authors sought to convey the impression that Hearst was not whole-heartedly for the vigorous prosecution of the war.

These garbled quotations made Hearst appear to say what he never said; and sometimes there were deleted expressions which, omitting vital sections of the quoted paragraphs, gave exactly the opposite meaning to what the whole, unmutilated statement clearly indicated.

Thousands got these lying pamphlets, who read and never sought to verify—thousands who never dreamed the source, who never stopped to ask where the money came from that financed the cost of printing and distribution; thousands who never could, by any possibility, hark back to the files, of dates long gone by, and who swallowed these infamous libels as gospel truth.

It's Up To You Mr. Reader

THE Hearst papers exposed the Standard Oil corruption by publishing the Archbold letters; secured evidence convicting the New York Central of giving secret rebates; defeated the New York Central's plan to grab Riverside Park; defeated the Southern Pacific Railway's Rockaway Park deal.

That is why these predatory interests all attack Hearst, who is working, not for his own pocket, but for the PUBLIC INTERESTS.

Are you for Hearst, or for the predatory interests?

One patriotic body whose members received these malicious pamphlets was about to take a vote censuring Hearst and the Hearst newspapers—in accordance with the printed request that accompanied the pamphlet in the mail—when an individual who was a constant reader of the Hearst newspapers asked that an impartial judge be selected to investigate the truth or falsity of the charges and report, before the organization put itself on record.

This organization was located miles away from New York. The judge, selected to look into the charges contained in *The Tribune's* pamphlet, was a lawyer, who had never read the Hearst papers. He came to New York and got a year's file, making twelve bound volumes. These were sent to his law office in another state. He studied the papers for weeks, reading editorials, digging into the news, noting the way the war especially was played, and the manner in which the cartoons were displayed.

After an exhaustive study he reported to his body that the Hearst newspapers were the most ardently American, loyal, patriotic publications it had ever been his good fortune to read. If anything, he said, naively, they were too rampantly American in tone to suit the sentiment of some of our allies. · His report created something of a sensation in that particular body for which he had made the investigation. The vote of censure was indignantly ruled out.

But what this solitary individual was able to do, few, if any, of the thousands upon thousands who received these pamphlets, through the mail, could do. The lies were gulped down wholesale and the propaganda was in full swing.

CONGRESS INVESTIGATES THE LEAGUE.

IT was at its height when Congress decided to investigate the activities of the National Security League which, during the political campaign of 1918, had amazed the nation by flooding the country with a statement, branding no less than 300 public men, mostly in Congress, as disloyal!

The League published its notorious "chart," consisting of a tabulated vote upon seven or eight measures that had come before Congress—the greater number of which were discussed in the House before we entered the war—and which set of votes was regarded as "the acid test" by which a Congressman was to be considered "loyal" or "disloyal."

As it turned out, upon investigation, the "acid test" really decided whether or not the Congressman had been loyal to the interests behind the National Security League, and not whether he had been loyal to the President, his country or the people.

Why Morgan Is Against Hearst

UPON calling the roll of eminent backers of the National Security League, we find answering to his name, among the contributors to the $1,000,000 " war fund," our old friend Morgan.

It was the Morgan firm of bankers who stood " to clean up " some millions of easy money, in preferential payment, in connection with the dual subway contract. Hearst put his cleverest lawyers on the job, and, after an action in court, legally separated the bankers from this juicy financial fat.

Morgan was the fiscal agent of Great Britain before we entered the war. Hearst's pronounced, almost rabid Americanism, at times, does not satisfy some of the reactionary elements in the government of Great Britain. **Morgan, who made millions in handling loans for Great Britain, b**efore our entrance into the war, naturally reflects this feeling of the British reactionaries against Hearst.

Do you wonder why Morgan and the National Security League are opposed to Hearst?

© J.P.MORGAN

Head of the big banking firm in Wall Street, who "gave up" to the huge fund of the National Security League. He has made many millions out of the big war.

(Continued from preceding page.)

CONGRESSMAN JAMES A. FREAR was one of those who had been branded as " disloyal " by this self-constituted band of patriots. **He had given two boys to the cause of Uncle Sam in the great war—the only two he had—and one of them died in France.**

The charge of disloyalty rankled in his heart. He found there were others, like himself, whose kin were in the war; **and one man, a member of Congress, was actually at the front, fighting in the trenches,** while these lip patriots, paid propagandists of the League, were going about his district branding him a traitor.

Congressman Frear decided to ask Congress to make an investigation and challenge the League to submit its proofs. Frear, in speaking for the support of his resolution, to probe the League said:

" No organized German propaganda during the war gave more comfort and aid to the enemy than the so-called Security League's efforts to create discord at home by besmirching our people generally or to encourage the foe abroad by charging the American Congress with disloyalty.

" **This junker corporation, outrivalling anything in Prussia, is the last word in un-Americanism.**

"LIKE RUTHLESS HUNS"

" **Like Huns who ruthlessly destroyed the homes of Belgians, these maligners of men and destroyers of reputations in time of war, can gloat over injuries inflicted on patriotic representatives with honored names, more treasured than gold or worldly goods, names which have been dragged in the mire by these character assassins.**

What is, or was—now that it seems to have sunk beneath the weight of public censure— this body called the National Security League?

© CONGRESSMAN FREAR

of Wisconsin, who started the probe that tore the mask of hypocrisy from the National Security League. He gave two sons to Uncle Sam, and one died in the service. And yet these lip patriots branded him as disloyal!

It is right that you people who have heard these calumnies about Hearst should know fully the character of these men who set out to destroy a whole Congress, because 300 of its members did not vote to suit the corporate masters behind the League; and who planned likewise to exterminate, if possible, the great American publisher whose pitiless journalistic guns poured such deadly shot into the ranks of exploiting wealth—the wealth this organization served.

S. STANWOOD MENKEN, the first president of the National Security League, said, on the witness stand, before the probers, that the inspiration for its organization came to him one day as he sat in the House of Commons in London.

Indeed, as we follow his story, told under oath, this ruthless organization of corporation controlled agents, seems to have come into the world, in anything but an American atmosphere. **Lawyers representing British connections and corporation agents attached to English houses of trade seemed to have been present at its birth.**

As we go along we shall see, here and there, in active, executive control, men who make their millions by British trade and leading lights of universities whose Anglomania is so extreme that it reflects, at times, seriously upon all that we have been taught to revere regarding the early history of our republic.

Mr. Menken, himself, admitted, as a starter, that he represented the London & Liverpool & Globe Assurance Company. He, likewise, admitted that the League which, at first, had said some nice things about Hearst, came to dislike the publisher because of **" what was regarded as an anti-British " strain in its editorial make-up,** and which became offensive because of Hearst's insistence upon the sentiment of " America First," as indicated in various ways in all the Hearst newspapers.

Among those most active in promoting the League—the men who assisted in ushering it into the world—were Frederic B. Coudert, who, he said, represented the British Government, as attorney; Joseph H. Choate, formerly Ambassador to Great Britain; Francis Vinton Greene, who was interested in the Canadian end of developing power from Niagara Falls, and J. G. White, an engineer employed by foreign governments.

When pressed as to his own connections, this man, who said the inspired idea of the League had come to him in the House of Commons, in England, admitted that he had many corporations among the list of his own clients. They were so many that he could not recall them all. He refused to name some of the largest, pleading privilege, but volunteered the information that he ministered to the great Tailer, Van Cortlandt and Cutter estates in this city, and represented the Cuban Sugar Mills, tobacco, steel, street railway, gas, realty and other corporations.

It was from such a man, with such connections, that the baby organization sprung and naturally it grew, and vigorously, upon the food that was fed to it through the willing channels of corporate contributions.

Menken remained as head of the National Security League until, one day, when off guard, he allowed himself to say something praiseworthy of Hearst. This inadvertence on his part so riled the corporation backers of the League that he was practically kicked out of the presidency and his place was taken by " Colonel " Charles E. Lydecker.

A FEATHER-BED "COLONEL"

" COLONEL " LYDECKER is not a real colonel. While the heroes of this great war were fighting their way up the slopes of Chauteau-Thierry, hacking their way through the Argonne, and suffering the tortures of Hell in the trenches, under the rain of German guns, our brave Colonel was busy, ever here, denouncing, as " disloyal," men who were serving the colors, and others whose sons were dying in France.

" Colonel " Lydecker was what you might call " a feather-bed " soldier. He did all his fighting 3,000 miles away from danger. If what the newspapers say he admitted at the time is true, he was something of a " slacker " in the Spanish-American War. Although a

" Boy Died in War, yet they called me Disloyal!"
—Frear

CONGRESSMAN JAMES A. FREAR, of Wisconsin, who introduced the resolution to have the political activities of the National Security League investigated, was among those attacked as "disloyal" by the self-constituted patriots in the League. Congressman Frear said:

"The only two boys I have, volunteered, and one of them, now, sleeps beneath the sod of France.

"And this League calls me disloyal!"

member of the National Guard of New York, he did not go into active service at that time; and his title of "Colonel," he said, was secured through action of the Governor, rather than through any daring deeds of military valor.

Let us show you how "Colonel" Lydecker's League worked—how it spread infamous untruths about patriotic men, and, at the same time, impudently refused to recant.

ARGONNE HERO BRANDED DISLOYAL

THERE was a Congressman named Royal Johnson, of South Dakota. This man was one of those who believed that the men who declare war ought to be willing to go to war. He left his seat in Congress, and a wife and three children—one of the latter an infant in arms—to enlist as a private soldier.

Congressman Johnson might have pulled wires and secured a commission and hid behind the safety of a swivel chair. But he did nothing of the kind. He marched away, a lowly man in the ranks, got into the fight on the other side and went through that grueling fire, in which our boys were trapped in the forest of Argonne.

He came home, the other day, limping his way on crutches, the result of a wound sustained in that terrible battle.

While Johnson was away, fighting for this country, Colonel Lydecker's League was busy, up and down the district, and throughout the land, spreading the statement that this brave soldier was "disloyal."

Representative Reavis, one of the probers, said to Lydecker, as the latter hung his head, on the witness stand:

"Your acid test held this brave man up before the country as disloyal. Knowing of this assault, now, don't you feel a little bit contemptible?"

Here is what Lydecker answered:

"I have no reproaches, whatever, to make against myself."

What will the men who fought through the Argonne, with Johnson, say to this?

What will the brave boys who fought in every battle, from Chateau-Thierry to Sedan, reply, when they read this burning insult uttered by the smug, swivel chair artist who says in the face of the figure on crutches: "I have no reproaches whatever to make against myself"?

Johnson may have voted in favor of some measure that would have cut a fat slice out of the graft of Lydecker's corporate masters. The fact that he had bled in one of the bloodiest fights of the war, could not, in the plutocratic eyes of Lydecker's backers, blot out the black fault that he had voted against them.

This is the organization that sought to defame Hearst!

This is the crowd that branded 300 men in public life as disloyal!

They have no "reproaches" to make against themselves.

What do YOU think of them readers?

Hero of Argonne, Back on Crutches, Branded as Disloyal!

AT A DYING WIFE'S BEDSIDE

ANOTHER instance of the League's injustice was that of Congressman Henry A. Barnhart, Democrat of Indiana. Barnhart was a victim of one of the League's most unscrupulous attacks. He had been held up for public condemnation on the charge that he "dodged the issue" in not voting for one of the measures approved by Lydecker's crowd.

The fact was that, at the time he was branded as disloyal and "dodging," Barnhart was at the bedside of his dying wife. He had taken the precaution to request leave of the

© W. K. VANDERBILT
Owner of the New York Central, which tried to grab the whole upper West Side of Manhattan. He is one of the backers of the National Security League.

Vanderbilt whose Railroad Hearst Halted in Big Land Grab

AMONG the contributors to the $1,000,000 "war fund" of the National Security League we discovered the name of William K. Vanderbilt.

Mr. Vanderbilt is one of the owners of the New York Central lines and allied railroad interests.

Hearst is the gentleman who exposed the attempt of the New York Central to grab the whole upper west side of the exceedingly valuable little island of Manhattan. All the New York Central wanted was a 6-track freight line through the city's parks, and a four-track elevated freight railroad through the streets of down-town Manhattan.

An expert, whom Hearst employed, said that this little favor which the New York Central wanted from the city was EASILY WORTH $30,000,000. Hearst put an awful kink in this plan and it didn't go through.

(Continued from preceding page.)

House, which had been granted unanimously. His wife died a few days after the vote was taken on the measure for "dodging" which he was censured.

As Barnhart faced the committee and told his story the flood of memory carried him back to the scene at the death bed of her he had loved in life. His voice became choked with emotion and he was unable, for some time, to go on. There was not a dry eye among those who heard this dramatic recital of a man who had been cruelly wronged.

Before leaving the stand, he said:

"**And they were attacking my patriotism, when two of my boys—the only two I have—were in the uniform of their country, one in the Regular Army and the other in the National Guard of Indiana.**"

Something cropped out, on the questioning of one Charles D. Orth, which gives a side light into this question of voting and how the League decided whether men were "loyal" or "disloyal."

WHO THE LEAGUE'S "LOYAL" MEN WERE

ORTH was the Chairman of the Committee on Congress for the League. Representative Harrison was questioning Orth, when Mr. Reavis, also one of the probers, brought out the fact that many of the League's "Roll of Honor" Congressmen, **had voted against measures which would have made the big interests, receiving tremendous war profits, bear the greater burden of the war's expenses.** Mr. Reavis showed that these "lily white supermen," in Congress, had voted against increasing income taxes to provide necessary war revenues.

"Your 'honor roll' men," said Reavis, "voted for measures which would tax the people of America, to put more money into the overloaded pockets of the munition magnates, and yet 40 per cent. of these men, whom your organization endorsed as voting 'right' opposed taking war profits to pay the expenses of the war."

Orth, on further examination by Congressman Browne, admitted that he had close business connections with British trade. He, himself, had lived in England for four years. His firm, Hanson & Orth, hemp importers, maintains an office in London. The witness admitted he was a director of the National Resin, Oil and Size Company, and the Pennsylvania & Delaware Oil Company. He was agent of the Mexican Sisal concerns, and had sold large quantities of hemp to the International Harvester Corporation. His firm, it developed, owned as high as 400 shares of stock in the Harvester Corporation.

Orth is a splendid specimen of the biased capitalistic captains of industry who backed and directed the affairs of the National Security League. His admissions on the stand went far to show that the League's only real purpose was to "get hunk" with all who stood in the way of the iron heel of capitalistic greed.

Before he left the stand he was forced to admit that the "chart" which his committee sent broadcast, showing 300 Congressmen "disloyal," and only 40 "loyal," was calculated to spread the belief that Congress was not behind the President, and therefore not back of the war "—and that this "would have given aid and comfort to the enemy."

When asked if this wouldn't have been the interpretation placed upon it by any spy into whose hands it should fall, Orth was forced to say " yes."

THE LEAGUE'S "POISON SQUAD"

THE League had a "poison squad," consisting, for the most part, of "leading educators," professors in universities, whose business it was to go about the country spreading the corrupt propaganda of their corporate masters, by means of lectures and missionary work among other college men.

Professor William H. Hobbs, of the University of Michigan, was in charge of the Ann Arbor Branch of the work. Congressman Browne brought out the fact that Professor Hobbs had said: **" It is inconceivable that the Ally premiers have invited President Wilson to visit Europe WHEN THEY KNOW HE IS PRO-GERMAN."** It was also shown that Professor Hobbs had written an article, **in which he declared the United States casualty lists had been padded " to give the President more influence in Europe."**

When these insults, hurled at the President of the United States, were repeated to Menken on the stand, and the former head of the League was asked what he thought of Professor Hobbs, the cagey Mr. Menken replied " There is wisdom in silence."

Ⓒ DR ROBT. MᶜNUTT MᶜELROY

One of the Security League's " poison squad." He went about the country lecturing for the League and called an audience in Wisconsin " a crowd of damned traitors," although there were men who wore the United States uniform and women present.

DR. ROBERT' McNUTT McELROY, formerly of Princeton, but later put in charge of the League's "educational activities," was another who went about the country insulting people. He appeared to speak before an audience in Wisconsin, and, because his hearers refused to applaud the spew of calumny which he hurled forth, **he called the audience " a crowd of damned traitors."**

Nice language, wasn't it, for an "educator," who was supposed to carry, with him, some of the polish of a great university!

INSULTED SOLDIERS AND WOMEN

Why even a Tammany thug, in the worst days of Tweed or Croker, wouldn't express himself, in that kind of language, before an audience. **And this audience, which Professor McElroy called " a crowd of damned traitors," contained men wearing the uniform of the United States Army, as well as respectable and cultured women,** whose ears had to bear the assault of this profane billingsgate.

McElroy, it developed, at the hearing, was paid $10,000 a year, by the National Security League, to do this sort of work. Can there be any luck in that sort of money? Is there any limit to what some men will stoop to do for such pay? Isn't Professor McElroy ashamed of the spectacle he has made of himself? Is Princeton proud of this product of corrupt and contemptible capitalistic coin?

All these things, friends, we are taking from the record. These statement are all to be found spread upon the minutes in the testimony of those who appeared before the congressional committee.

Some of these things—this appalling denunciation of the President of the United States as "a pro-German," an accusation dangerously akin to a charge of high treason and which, if true, would seem to call for impeachment—appear to us, as we go over the findings, to be hardly believable. We marvel that these men dared to say and to do the things, it is admitted, upon investigation, that they did and said, in the mad moments of war hysteria, and when the mere whisper of suspicion was enough to incite an inflamed populace to acts of deadly violence.

THIS ONE PRAISED ENGLISH TORIES

ANOTHER "leading educator," of the League's propaganda squad, who went about denouncing men as "disloyal," was Professor Claude H. Van Tyne, of the University of Michigan.

The Congressional committee found out that Professor Van Tyne had written a book. It was entitled, "The Loyalists in the American Revolution." Professor Van Tyne, "loyal" patriot, called it, in a sub-caption, "an appreciation of the Tories in the American Revolution, and their Persecution by the colonists."

Understand, gentle reader, that these same colonists were none other than our immortal patriot, George Washington, and his devoted band of followers, who suffered all the horrors of war and famine, in such places as Valley Forge. The Tories were those who sympathized with England, and who were sworn, in large part, to hand Washington over to King George, in the event of his capture, and have him hanged as a rebel and a traitor to the Mother country.

Among other things, Professor Van Tyne, in his book, defending the Tories, said: "The Loyalists were conservative, sober-minded men to whom posterity may conceive the character of patriots."

But this un-American feature of the National Security League, so brazenly transparent on the record, was not the worst characteristic. It was when the investigating committee began to go behind the record and call for the names of the donors to the big "slush" fund of $1,000,000 that the real nature of this corrupt band of character assassins became revealed in all its many sordid sides.

THE BIG "SLUSH" FUND OF THE LEAGUE

EARLY in the war William Jennings Bryan was quoted as branding the National Security League as the paid agent of the munitioneers and shipping interests. The League, then about to launch upon its career of vilification and false accusations, hurriedly called in an auditor "to prove that its funds came from uncontaminated sources," and particularly to show "that no contributions were made by or expected in the interests of munition workers or others financially interested in the declaration of war."

THE CONGRESSMEN FOUND THIS TO BE A HIDEOUS FALSEHOOD!

One by one the probers dragged from unwilling lips the names of profiteer after profiteer —men whose firms had piled up millions out of the war; uncovered one after another, the men who had grown fabulously rich, over night, whose names had figured in Wall Street sensations, time and again, and whose record of exploitation, for the most part, is a blot upon the pages of American economic history.

Steel kings, powder kings, copper kings, money kings—all the robber barons of the great commercial highway, were lined up behind this organization, with their millions, ready to bludgeon, amid the hysteria of war, all those who had assailed or attempted to expose their iniquities, in the past. Ominously, in the background, were the two great menacing shadows of corrupting corporate wealth—the Rockefeller and Carnegie Foundations.

Speaking of these two great corporate menaces, Hearst has said:

"We are beginning to learn the truth about these great foundations. They are not employed and were never created for the purpose of serving the public, but for the purpose

(Continued on page 21.)

Why Mackay Opposes Hearst

CLARENCE H. MACKAY, who owns the big telegraph and cable company, is one of the prominent contributors to the "war fund" of the National Security League, which unmercifully assailed Hearst and some three hundred congressmen.

Mackay is now fighting the effort of the government to take over the concern which enjoys a monopoly in handling telegraph and cable tolls.

Hearst, it will be remembered, has been hammering at this monopoly for a long time. He believes the government, in this country, ought to handle the wire business as do the governments on the other side of the ocean.

There is a reason for the National Security League's animosity to Hearst.

of serving the individuals and the class which founded them; and like certain kept colleges are maintained by subsidy to spread the doctrine of special privilege and to attack, to misrepresent and, as far as possible, to discredit the supporters of popular liberties and true democracy."

"In other words, these great Foundations are the foes of the public, the enemies of popular rights, the persistent and powerful agents of the privileged classes in maintaining their unjust privileges and in slandering the public servants who believe in equal rights and equal opportunities and who oppose special privileges."

PROFITEERS AND THE MILLIONS THEY MADE

LOOK at the list of contributors to the immense "slush" fund of the National Security League, and then study carefully the millions which these men coined from the blood of 8,000,000 victims in this war!

J. P. MORGAN, the head of the great banking firm in Wall Street, who acted as the fiscal agent for Great Britain before we entered the war, and whose concern made millions out of the early loans. The Morgans are financial agents of most of the great monopolistic corporations in the world. Their ramifications extend from one side of the world to the other. They have gorged and fattened to unbelievable proportions upon the wrecks of over-capitalized concerns. Morgan, himself, is a director in seven of the largest corporations in the United States, including United States Steel. After paying all taxes, in 1917, the Steel Corporation's net profits were $244,738,906!

JOHN D. ROCKEFELLER, whose corporation connections, growing out of the strangle hold which Standard Oil exercises in every direction, makes him one of the most powerful figures, in the capitalistic world, donated $35,000 to the fund. The profits made in gasoline, during the period of the war, when petrol was at a premium in Europe, and the millions reaped in kerosene oil, during the shortage in coal, are said to be such as to stagger the imagination!

NICHOLAS F. BRADY, chief owner of the Brooklyn Rapid Transit, whose company, exploited to the limit of capitalistic cupidity, was recently thrown into the hands of a receiver, after a disaster—the Malbone Tunnel wreck—in which a hundred lives were snuffed out in an instant. Brady is a director in 50 large corporations, including the United States Rubber Company. The pre-war profits of this concern were about $5,000,000. Its average yearly war profits were $11,000,000, or EXCESS PROFITS, DURING THE WAR, OF SIX MILLION DOLLARS!

ARTHUR CURTIS JAMES—Multi-millionaire, and enormously wealthy because of his connection, as one of the heads of the Smelters' Trust, known as The American Smelting & Refining Company, which benefited prodigiously by the war. He gave $40,000! James is vice-president of the Phelps-Dodge Company, whose excess war profits averaged $14,531,864 a year!

H. H. ROGERS, son and heir of the late Standard Oil organizer, who is a director in the Amalgamated and Anaconda Copper Companies. The Anaconda's excess war profits were given at $46,200,642!

CHARLES HAYDEN, a director of 26 corporations, was a heavy contributor. One of his concerns, The Nevada Consolidated Copper Company, benefited from the war to the extent of $11,354,000! Another, the Utah Copper Company, reaped excess profits of $32,005,240 a year during the war!

H. C. FRICK, director of the United States Steel Corporation, which took profits of nearly $250,000,000 during the war, and which is backed by the Carnegie interests, was also a contributor. The Carnegie Foundation donated $150,000 toward the propaganda of the League!

CLARENCE H. MACKAY, head of the Postal Telegraph & Cable Company, which is violently opposed to the Government plan to take over the wire business of the country. Mackay is particularly aggrieved at Hearst's unceasing fight for government ownership.

WILLIAM K. VANDERBILT, one of the owners of the New York Central lines, and allied railroad interests, tied up with the Mills Estate, owners of The Tribune, and others in the efforts of this road to grab the upper west side of Manhattan, and whose road has opposed all efforts of the citizens to end the maintenance of "Death Avenue," the street, at grade, along which the New York Central runs its tracks through the crowded heart of lower Manhattan. So terrible has this menace to life become in New York, that the citizens have organized a society grimly known as "The League to End Death Avenue."

T. COLEMAN DU PONT, head of the du Pont de Nemours Company, the great Munitions Trust, whose profits during the war, by the sale of explosives, became so enormous that many now believe his wealth challenges even that of the Rockefellers for world supremacy. The fabulous profits of the du Ponts, whose wealth leaped to staggering proportions, practically over night, is one of the stupendous developments of this terrible traffic in the tragedy of world war! It is whispered that the powder king cannot calculate within millions of his enormous holdings.

WHY SHOULD ANYONE FATTEN ON WAR?

Shouldn't these staggering figures of profits, reaped from the blood of millions maimed and slain on the field of battle, give us pause, and lead us to contemplate the enormity of this shameful traffic? Why should any individual, or group of individuals, be privileged to enjoy a monopoly in this bloody business? Why should any solitary man, in the United States, or elsewhere, be permitted to fatten upon this hideous trade?

Bad enough for governments to have to go to war, particularly when one is forced into a world cataclysm such as ours was compelled to enter—but why should that tragic event be made the means of enriching any one man beyond the wildest dreams of avarice?

While we are on the subject of fat fortunes, built up in this way, let us take a look at some of the statistics of the great war.

The latest figures show that the total cost of the war, to both sides was $179,000,000,000, of which amount our country, alone, spent $18,481,000,000.

Grasp, if you can, the meaning of these figures—the money subscribed gladly by the people to bring victory to our flag—and then realize the millions scooped in by profiteers, who hid behind the mask of this character-destroying National Security League, who lay

JOHN D. ROCKEFELLER

Founder of the Standard Oil Trust, which Hearst. exposed years ago, by documentary evidence, as one of the agencies purchasing Senators at Washington and corrupting Legislation.

Rockefeller and the Standard Oil Letters—"This man's wealth a menace to nation" says Hearst.

AFTER looking down the list of prominent contributors to the $1,000,000 fund of the National Security League, our eye lights with cordial recognition, upon the familiar name of Rockefeller.

This is our old friend of the Standard Oil Trust.

Hearst, once upon a time, secured excellent photographic copies of some letters which an official of the Standard Oil Company had sent to various United States Senators. Each one began "My dear Senator," gave explicit instructions how to vote, killing certain measures which the Standard Oil did not want enacted into law, and then closed with this very illuminating sentence: "**Enclosed you will find certificate for $25,000, which I have deposited to your credit.**" Hearst went around the country, reading these letters to huge and delighted audiences; Rockefeller considered it anything but clubby. The letters exposed the hand of the Standard Oil at the throat of government. Do you wonder why Rockefeller and the National Security League are opposed to Hearst?

(Continued from preceding page.)

in wait behind the ambush of war madness to destroy those whom they hated, and who reaped these frightful profits while the flower of the nations went forth to die.

And how many, do you think, died in this great war?

The total list of killed, on all the battlefields, on both sides, has been officially reported as 7,909,768—which does not take into consideration those who died of disease, were maimed, wounded or captured and which number amounts to 19,524,989, additional, or a grand total of 27,434,757 for the casualties on both sides in the world war, that has just drawn to a close.

Of the 7,909,768 killed, the Central Powers lost, 3,350,000, and the Allies 4,559,768. Germany lost 2,600,000 and Austria 800,000. Among the Allies, Russia was the heaviest loser, heading the list with 1,700,000; France came next with 1,400,000 and Great Britain, including all her colonies lost 658,000. The number of killed for the United States is listed at 73,000, with 264,998, dead of disease, wounded or missing.

This is the tale which the figures tell of the frightful toll, which death, disease and devastation took in the great conflict.

EIGHT MILLION LIVES!

And feeding upon that scene of carnage were the human vultures who have come out of it enormously rich—proud and insolent and vindictive in their new-found polluted wealth, and hot for further spoil!

These war-fed plunderers, risen to new heights of power, now seek to destroy all who stand in their way, in the last assault on the few liberties that still remain to the people.

Woe to the man who still seeks to stay their money mad lust—to the man who still essays to play the role of champion for the oppressed, who seeks to voice the widespread indignation of the exploited masses!

With this massed menace of wealth behind them they seek to rend and tear, like human tigers, all the helpless and the hopeless in the jungle of a disordered civilization.

This National Security League, and the terrible figures of corrupt wealth behind it, are what bring on and breed Bolshevism!

Louis, the Bourbon, said: "After us the deluge!"

The munitioneers and powder kings of the National Security League have said:

"After us, the explosion!"

Becker's Brazen Story About Bolo

Tried to create impression that French spy had come here to meet Hearst when he had hidden Documentary proof that man came to America to do business with J. P. Morgan—Whole story built upon false charges of an ex-convict.

PERHAPS the most amazing, and luridly sensational, story circulated by the agents of the interests opposed to Hearst, and one that attracted attention on both sides of the water, because of the prominence of the personages mentioned in the tale, was that sprung by one Alfred L. Becker, a defeated candidate for public office, who tried to create the impression that Bolo Pasha had come to this country, purposely to meet Hearst. Bolo has since been shot as a traitor to France.

Becker went all the way to Washington, to tell this startling story to a congressional committee. The fact that Becker was, at that time, holding office as Deputy Attorney General of the State of New York lent some dignity to the witness and gave his story an official coloring. It was immediately taken up by the subsidized press, and spread to every corner of the country.

It was not until Senator James A. Reed, who was a member of the General Committee, of which the investigating committee was a sub-committee, took an interest in the proceedings, and began to question Becker, that **one of the most brazen plots ever conceived was laid bare in all its daring details.**

Reed, as he sat and listened to Becker glibly rattle off his story, became convinced that the man was an unconscionable liar. He learned that there had been a political campaign in the State of New York, in which Becker had become involved on the side of his chief, Attorney General Merton E. Lewis, who was a candidate for Governor in the Republican primaries against Governor Charles S. Whitman.

① ATTY. GEN BECKER

Here is the man who employed ex-convicts, one of them a confessed swindler, in an $800,000 fraud, to help in the plan to discredit Hearst. Senator Reed tore his story to pieces before the Senate Investigating Committee.

Becker and Lewis, in that campaign, **failing to get the support of the Hearst newspapers, spread a story to the effect that Hearst had met Bolo Pasha, when the latter came to this country.** They believed that this story would reflect seriously on Hearst and injure Whitman by indirection, inasmuch as, between the two candidates, the Hearst newspapers seemed to favor Whitman.

Hearst, however, compelled Lewis to apologize and later admit that an investigation of Bolo's movements, at the time he was visiting here, showed that Hearst had only the most casual kind of an acquaintance with the man, and, indeed, had met him at a dinner given publicly at Sherry's, which was attended by others, all of pronounced Allied sympathies, and that all believed Bolo to be what he pretended, then, to be—an ardent French patriot.

BECKER and Lewis, in the political campaign which followed the first appearance of this story, were both defeated. **Becker, who was a candidate for Attorney General to succeed his boss, Lewis, was overwhelmingly swamped and he attributed this defeat to Hearst.**

He winced under this defeat. He vowed "to get hunk." He admitted later, under grilling cross-examination, by Senator Reed, that the compelling motive in making public the statements about Hearst and Bolo, was a political one. He chose what he thought was an auspicious moment to resurrect the old story which has been used in his own political campaign, but which had been killed by the apology of Lewis. He pretended to have additional matter which ought to be laid before the congressional committee.

Had Becker succeeded in doing what he wished to do, in the plan of revenge which he mapped out for himself, he would have told his story in a certain way, using only Hearst's name in the recital, carefully covered up the sources of his information, giving the impression that the "evidence" was gathered by special "secret experts," whose identity "could not be disclosed," and would have gone back to New York thoroughly satisfied with having done a proper and splendid job.

But Senator Reed smashed all that neat little plan to smithereens, as, presently, you shall see.

As Becker had made a great sensation out of the story that Bolo came to America specially to meet Hearst, and as the latter had declared he had never even heard of Bolo before he came to these shores, and then had agreed to meet him with others, only because Bolo was reported to be a great publisher, like himself, **Reed became determined to find out whom it was that Bolo really DID come here to meet.**

BOLO CAME HERE TO MEET MORGAN

AND then something popped out in the evidence which created a real sensation, something which Becker had never intended to disclose.

Bolo, the French traitor, who had been shot as a spy, and with whose name Becker was trying hard to link that of Hearst's, it developed, came here really to meet none other than J. P. Morgan, of the big banking firm in Wall Street.

This was established, unquestionably, by the production of documentary evidence—the strongest sort of proof—that Bolo Pasha came to New York to do business with the Morgan firm, and that he wanted credits amounting to the unusual sum of $1,000,000!

One of these documents, a telegram, cabled by the Paris branch of the Morgan firm, of which Baron Harjes is the head, and which established

BOLO PASHA

Bolo Pasha, the French traitor, shot as a spy, who came to this country with letters of introduction to J. P. Morgan (which fact Becker hid), and whom the Morgan firm was ready to lend a million dollars! Becker, who tried to link Hearst's name with that of the spy's, was flabbergasted when Reed dug up the Morgan connection!

Why Did Becker Hide Morgan's Name ?

All the time Becker was telling his false story about Hearst, he knew that Bolo Pasha, the spy, really came here to meet the Morgans. There was documentary evidence to this effect, hidden for seventeen months. Why did Becker seek to hide this fact?

Where "J.P.M." Put His "O.K." to Bolo

(Continued from preceding page.)

beyond the scintilla of a doubt the real reason for Bolo coming to America, was found by the Attorney General of New York himself among the files of the Morgan firm. **And yet, his office tried to give the impression that Bolo had come here to meet Hearst, when, as a matter of fact, he knew all along—was possessed of a cablegram that told the truth—that this was not so!**

What do you think, readers, of that for a piece of duplicity? Note the evident care to cover up the profiteering house of Morgan, and the unusual effort to besmirch the name of Hearst. This is how the hand of capitalism plays the game—always with loaded dice.

This cablegram was sedulously kept from the public eye for over seventeen months, and became public only when it was dragged into the light through the investigation into Becker's startlingly false story about Hearst. Those who seek to do evil to others always overreach themselves, and sooner or later the truth about every man, falsely assailed, comes forth to undo his false accusers.

A T the time of Bolo Pasha's visit to New York, and long before he was suspected as a spy, dealing with German agents, the head of the Morgan firm enjoyed the closest confidential relations with both the French and English governments. Morgan was their fiscal agent he had floated their big loans before we entered the war He was supposed to know all the secrets—to be able to spot, at a glance, the false from the true, the loyal from the treacherous.

☉ JEROME (EX-CONVICT)

(Rogues Gallery picture)
Arrested Sept. 12, 1908, charged with grand larceny. Pleaded guilty to extortion and sentenced, February 8, 1909, to four years in Sing Sing. Was one of those used by Becker to make false affidavit against Hearst.

If Morgan didn't know that Bolo was a spy; if he was willing to do business with him and personally " O. K." his credit, placing the magic initials " J. P. M." on the letter of introduction (also found in the investigation) and thus giving the Frenchman a clean bill—how in the world was Hearst, who knew Bolo only slightly, a mere handshaking acquaintance, to know that he was anything but what he pretended to be—a patriot who ardently loved France?

Can't you see the injustice, the enormity of this attempted " frame-up," in Becker's sensational Bolo story, told, at first so glibly and damagingly to the committee—until Reed began to dig for the evidence behind the plot?

HAD LETTERS FROM MORGAN'S PARIS BANK

The Paris agents of Morgan thought so highly of Bolo that they gave him splendid letters of recommendation, written by Baron Harjes himself.

"We think it perhaps well to add," writes the Baron, "in view of the somewhat Oriental sonance of this gentleman's name and title, that he is not a Turk, and, in fact, is the brother of a well-known French Archbishop."

Again, on June 9, 1916, the Paris office wires to J. P. Morgan & Co., in New York, that Bolo's "connections are of great importance to us." The cable reads:

"Bolo Pasha says: 'Remit us, cable his balance.' Would be very pleased if you could allow some interest, possibly even 2 per cent., in view of connections of this client, which of great importance to us."

U. S. SENATOR JAMES A. REED

United States Senator James A. Reed, who saw through the falsity of Becker's story and dragged from his unwilling lips the truth about the ex-convicts employed to " frame-up " affidavits in the sensational Bolo " case."

This was considered of such supreme importance that " J. P. M.," the big boss in Wall Street, attended to the job, personally, initialling it himself, and writing plainly the " 2 per cent." which Bolo was to receive.

How mighty is this king whose millions sway the empire of finance? No king, in ancient days, ever affixed a signature that meant more than the cryptic " J. P. M." placed at the corner of the Bolo cablegram. And yet it was the warrant royal that favored one who was afterward denounced as a spy.

To say that Becker was dumbfounded at the course his sensational Bolo story had taken, that he was chagrined at the manner in which the case had gotten away from him, would be putting it mildly, indeed.

WAS A BIG MAN IN FRANCE

OTHERS had met Bolo when he came to New York and yet it never occurred to Becker to suspect any of these. Bolo was so highly thought of, coming as he did the welcome representative of a beloved ally, that he was everywhere graciously received. He was dined and wined. He sat at table with noted dignitaries.

He was the brother of Monsignor Bolo, a distinguished prelate of the Roman Catholic Church in Paris and one of the most eloquent preachers in France; an intimate friend of Judge Monier, holding one of the highest judicial positions in France; the partner of Senator Humbert in the newspaper business; and his influence was sufficient to secure his invitation to a dinner of President Poincaire of France and of Louis Barthou, an ex-Premier of France.

© PHILIP MUSICA

Ex-convict, one of a gang of $800,000 bank swindlers, who defrauded government by short-weighing of imports. Pleaded guilty and was sentenced to a year and pay a fine of $5,000. His employment by Becker against Hearst was exposed in Congressional hearing. Was paid $10,000 of public funds for this work at Becker's instance.

Mr. Hearst, with seven or eight others, was invited to meet Bolo Pasha at dinner in the public dining room at Sherry's. The other guests included Jules Bois, the well-known French lecturer, who was then speaking in this country in behalf of the French Government: Julian Gerard, the brother of the then American Ambassador to Berlin, and Mr. Van Anda, the managing editor of the New York *Times.*

The conversation during the dinner in the public dining room of Sherry's was upon general topics. If anything of importance on any subject was said by Bolo Pasha to anybody or by anybody to him it escaped Mr. Hearst's notice. A published statement, written later by Mr. Van Anda, managing editor of the New York *Times,* indicates that his recollection of the dinner and the occasion and his understanding of the character of Bolo Pasha were the same as Mr. Hearst's.

During the dinner Bolo Pasha told Mr. Hearst that he was having difficulty in getting print paper for his Paris Journal and he desired to talk with him about obtaining a supply in America.

Three or four days later he called at Mr. Hearst's house. The object of his visit was to ascertain from Mr. Hearst, if possible, how he could obtain some print paper in this country. Mr. Hearst told him that he would have great difficulty in getting paper for export as the American publishers were having trouble in getting enough paper for home consumption. **Mr. Hearst's recollection is that he offered to give him a letter to the principal paper manufacturers, but after a brief chat upon conventional social topics, Bolo took his leave. Nothing of a private, or personal, or political nature was mentioned between them.**

ⓒ PERLEY MORSE

The expert accountant, who repudiated Becker, before the Senate Committee, and exposed the trick whereby Von Papen's and Boy-Ed's names were slipped into a false report against Hearst.

Mr. Hearst never saw Bolo Pasha afterwards or heard from him. He never at any time had any personal knowledge of his character, antecedents, or purposes, other than stated here. He does not remember to have heard even his name mentioned again until the exposure was made of his true character, about eighteen months later in Paris.

What do you know, Mr. Reader, about the inside life of half the men you meet every day, casually, in the course of business?

BECKER'S METHODS DISGUST PROBERS

LONG before Becker got half way through with his testimony **Major E. Lowry Humes, who was acting as attorney for the committee, practically admitted that " there had been very little competent testimony presented."**

Time and again Senators interjected questions which elicited the fact that Becker was going mainly upon suppositions of his own.

The character of his testimony, at this stage, was such that Senator Wolcott was moved to make a mighty protest.

IT was then developed that Becker had taken affidavits from bellboys, elevator men and hack drivers in an attempt to link Hearst's name with another noted character—this time Count Bernstoff. The manner in which those affidavits were taken roused the ire of Senator Reed.

Senator Reed—" At th ...ry moment when you took that deposition and that you swore these affidavits, and at the same time you wrote out the affidavits, on the same date, same hour, at same room, you had in mind that you were going to use the affidavits for a political purpose?"

Mr. Becker—" Unquestionably."

WHERE THE CASE BEGAN TO WEAKEN

IT was about this stage of the proceedings that Becker began to sense that Senator Reed was getting beneath his mask. The questioning led gradually to the sources from which Becker drew his information about the things which he had been so glibly testifying in regard to Hearst. Senator Reed thought it about time that the committee should have a look at some of this original information.

Becker began to wince. **It was one of the things he did not wish to disclose—the**

633

14001.

RECEIVED
J.P. MORGAN & CO. N.Y.
MAR 14 1916

The Royal Bank of Canada.

Corner William & Cedar Streets

G.L. 22

New York, March 14, 1916

CABLE ADDRESS "ROYALBANK"

R.E. JONES
J.R. BRUCE } AGENTS
H.S. HART ASSISTANT

Messrs. J. P. Morgan & Co.,

    23 Wall Street,

       New York City.

Gentlemen:-

    In accordance with instructions received from Mr Paul Bolo Pacha, we beg to hand you herewith our check for,

        $170,068.03

which kindly place to the credit of Senator Charles Humbert, of Paris, France

    Kindly sign the accompanying receipt and return same to bearer

        Yours very truly

        Pro Agent.

(Continued from preceding page.)

source of all this story which had been concocted about Hearst, which had been put together by hack drivers and bell boys, together in a room, and, in one instance, corrected "to make the date right."

    Reed wanted to know who got these characters together—what sinister influence was back of it all. One of the men used in the case was Jerome, the ex-convict. It was getting close to the last sordid act in this drama. Becker was beginning to stand forth in a drab light.

    Finally he decided to defy the committee and refuse to produce the records demanded by Reed.

    Mr. Becker—" They will not be produced; and I want to say now that I will not produce any of the confidential papers of our so-called secret service department, nor will I produce or give any information in regard to the personnel of the investigators who have been working for the department."

Becker was extremely anxious that the names of his informants should be kept secret. He hinted that they were important investigators whose work might be seriously crippled.

The more he tried to hedge the more insistent Reed became that Becker should produce the records. The committee became interested. The keenest curiosity became centered about the identity of these investigators "who had dug up the stuff on Hearst."

Becker played desperately for time. The web began to close about him. The committee decided he would have to produce. Then Becker, reluctantly, dragged forth, into the light of day, the source of all this information, the story by which he sought to defame Hearst.

The revelation shocked the committee. It roused the indignation of Reed. It appalled the public. It turned the last doubter into an ardent champion of Hearst.

THE EXPERT "INVESTIGATORS," THE "MEN" WHOSE ALL IM-PORTANT WORK MIGHT BE IMPEDED BY THE REVELATION OF THEIR IDENTITIES, WHOSE PERSONALITIES BECKER WAS SO IN-SISTENT UPON CONCEALING WAS FOUND TO BE AN EX-CONVICT!

An ex-convict, a man with the stigma of the prison cell upon him, stool pigeon of the underworld, to whom had been paid the money of the people, as Senator Reed discovered in the sum of ten thousand dollars!

Under a terrible, gruelling examination by Reed, it developed that a confessed larcenist, on parole from the Tombs, who had been involved in an $800,000 swindle, had procured and written with his own hand the affidavits which Becker used in an attempt to connect Hearst with the activities of Bolo Pasha.

PHILIP MUSICA, who spent three years in the Tombs upon his own confession of complicity in the notorious "hair fraud" cases, who had turned upon his co-partners in the crime, and been paroled after his testimony had been used to convict these accomplices, was the important figure whom Becker had so desperately tried to conceal.

There stood Musica, the swindler, with the odor of the Tombs about him, as the source of this story which, all had been led to believe, came as the result of the work of government secret service operatives on two continents!

Musica, working under two aliases, rounded up hack drivers, bell boys, elevator boys, and dragooned them into rooms, where they all sat and compared and corrected what they were to say!

The investigation into the Bolo Pasha case, as a matter of fact, it further developed to the great surprise of the committee, had nothing whatever to do with Hearst. In fact, Hearst was not even in question, when this international case was being investigated in New York.

This was an astounding admission. The public had been led to believe that whatever it was that Becker "had on Hearst," was something that developed as a result of secret evidence, secured under the letters rogatory in the Bolo Pasha case.

Senator Reed was so disgusted with the case, at this point, that he said:

"If this man Musica was employed in Becker's office and employed on this business, and is a convict and a notorious criminal, then that bears upon every act and every transaction that took place and bears upon the good faith of this entire transaction.

"The question of whether this man is a convict that was engaged in this business, goes to the very heart and soul of the whole matter."

CONVICT PAID WITH PEOPLE'S MONEY

It was at this point that Becker, beaten at every point, in the game of evidence, and helpless in the hands of Reed, made one last desperate play to hold back the story of what Musica, the confessed criminal, was paid for his services against Hearst.

Senator Reed—"I propose to show that Mr. Becker sent this convict out, knowing him to be a a convict, to get this evidence; that he connived with these witnesses; that he has been paid large sums of money through Mr. Becker's office, for his services; that he is on a salary down there, or was, of twenty dollars a day and expenses, I think."

And Senator Reed proceeded rapidly to show just how Musica had been used, what he had been paid and how.

It developed that Becker had taken Musica to his home, and had lived with him at the Murray Hill Hotel. He finally admitted that Musica was his friend and he "stood for him."

After this admission on the part of Becker, Senator Reed insisted on reading into the record the indictment in full, to which Musica, the convict, had confessed, when charged with complicity in the $800,000 fraud.

THE knock-out blow for Becker came, when Perley Morse, an expert public accountant, who had worked with Becker in the early part of the case, took the stand and repudiated this man, after hinting that records of some of his reports in the case had been tampered with and that an injection of Mr. Hearst's name, in one particular was a rank forgery.

Morse testified that he could not, in all conscientiousness, work any longer with Becker. He read from an entry in his diary of October 29, 1917, as follows:

" Mr. Morse concludes he could not work with Mr. Becker any longer, because he will get us all into trouble."

Becker asked Morse why he wrote that and the witness replied:

" If a man doesn't care to associate with ex-convicts, he has that privilege."

"WE MUST LAND THIS —— HEARST!"

That Becker was determined to get Hearst is shown by the story which Perley Morse told about the ex-convict Musica calling him on the telephone.

Mr. Morse—"First, Mr. Musica asked me over the telephone. It seems that this Mr. Johnson (Musica's alias), who is—I had better call him by his full name, so as not to mix him up with the other man—Severance Johnson. He was a man that had been connected with the Hearst publications. Musica called me up one afternoon and he said they were examining Severance Johnson, and he called me to come up and face him, because they might as well finish this man Hearst right away."

Senator Reed—" What was the term about Hearst? What did he call him?"

Mr. Morse—" It is the name that is not pronounced in polite society."

Senator Reed—" Tell us the language as near as you can, and you can omit this language."

Mr. Morse—" ' It is time that we land this —— Hearst.' I think I got Mr. Becker on the 'phone right away after that and told him that I did not approve of those methods, and I believe that I met Mr. Becker that night or the day after in the evening, and dined with him. I told him those methods would not succeed, and he should not do those things. I think I told him that you could not do that way in New York and succeed; that New York people would not stand for it. Mr. Becker was from Buffalo."

Morse then turned to where Becker sat and said:

" Mr. Becker, I warned Attorney-General Lewis against you way back in October, and also other friends of his warned Attorney-General Lewis against you at that time."

The revelations against Becker were such, at this point, that the case collapsed. The committee wanted to expunge the whole charge against Hearst from the record.

Senator Reed, however, insisted that it should stand as a monument to the infamous lengths to which Hearst's traducers had dared to go.

Speaking of Pro-German: Read This!

THE following was found in the files of a New York newspaper, and relates to the visit, to this country, a few years ago, of Prince Henry of Prussia, the brother of Kaiser Wilhelm (now known as Herr Hohenzollern):

" The rare honor, among the society leaders of this city, of entertaining the Kaiser's brother, has fallen to the Ogden Millses. at whose mansion, No. 2 East Sixty-ninth Street, the Prince was a guest, yesterday, from 1 o'clock until 3.

"Commodious as the great dining room, in the Mills residence, is, accommodations could not be afforded for more than sixty diners * * * * *. The event was rich and sumptuous * * * * *. For three days, workmen had been engaged in completing the decorations, and the house was a garden of exotics, when Prince Henry was welcomed.

' Thompson, the Mills chef, served the luncheon, and operatic and musical stars furnished the entertainment * * *. Mr. Ogden Mills sat directly opposite the princely guest at luncheon."

It seems, from this newspaper account, that there was great rivalry for the Prince's favor between the Millses and the Vanderbilts. The latter had secured the Kaiser's brother. all to themselves, until the Mills family got on the job, and got the wires to Berlin working.

" It may be safely assumed," says the reporter of that day, " that the Kaiser has had his say in this matter and that his sanction has been obtained to Prince Henry's presence at the Mills luncheon * * *. This is a notable departure from the very strict rule laid down by the Kaiser, in connection with the movements of his brother."

This can't, by any possibility, be the Mills family that owns The New York Tribune, eh? Imagine the Tribune toasting: " Hoch der Prinz!"

Ach! das war Schrecklich!

ELIHU ROOT—A BRIEF EPITOME of HIS CAREER

ELIHU ROOT is one of the prime movers in the attack upon Hearst. Root has been U. S. Senator, Secretary of War, and Secretary of State. But he has never held an elective office except delegate to a Constitutional Convention. He distrusts the people, has always refused to stand for election before the people, and as soon as U. S. Senators were elected by the people, he resigned. He is honorary President of The National Security League.

E. H. Harriman, the great railroad man, wrote in his famous letter to Sidney Webster:

"Ryan's success in all his manipulations, traction deals, tobacco combination, manipulation of the State Trust Company into the Morton Trust Company, the Shoe and Leather Bank into the Western National Bank and then again into the Bank of Commerce—thus covering up his tracks —has been done by the adroit mind of Elihu Root."

William C. Whitney, the head of the Metropolitan Street Railway Syndicate, praised Elihu Root in these words:

"I have had many lawyers who told me what we could not do and what the law forbade. Elihu Root is the first lawyer I ever had who could always tell me how to do legally what we wanted to do."

Root was one of the lawyers whose technical skill kept out of jail for three years the late William M. Tweed, the first man to loot New York City on a scale commensurate with its wealth and population. After his trial and conviction Judge Noah Davis, who presided at the trial, said to the Tweed lawyers, including Elihu Root, whom he mentioned by name:

"I ask you, gentlemen, to remember that good faith to a client never can justify or require bad faith to your own consciences, and that however good a thing it may be to be known as successful and great lawyers, it is even a better thing to be known as honest men."

Immediately after Tweed's conviction one of Tweed's houses appeared as Root's property. This was apparently Root's fee for defending Tweed.

Root's first appointive office was as U. S. District Attorney. While he was in office Jake Sharp procured the Broadway franchises from the Legislature by bribery and several "boodle" Aldermen were sent to the penitentiary.

ROOT TIES UP WITH A SWIFT CROWD

ROOT resigned his District Attorneyship to become counsel to William C. Whitney who, with Messrs. Widener, Dolan, Elkins, of Philadelphia, and Thomas F. Ryan, and Anthony N. Brady, of New York, then began the trafficking in franchises, street railways, gas and electric light companies in New York which made them all multi-millionaires.

The Broadway franchise, whose purchase sent several Aldermen to the penitentiary, Root bought for Ryan at a receiver's sale for $25,000. De Lancey Nicoll, who had prosecuted the "boodle"

ELIHU ROOT

The brains behind all the big franchise grabs in New York in the last 25 years! The man who showed Whitney, Brady, Widener, Elkins and others how to exploit New York and laugh at the impotent wrath of its people!

31

Aldermen, then became the personal attorney of Ryan, as Root was the personal attorney of Whitney. Nicoll was a Democrat, Root a Republican.

The Syndicate thus controlled the County Chairmen and the "Bosses" of both parties. Whichever party won an election, the Syndicate always kept its servants in office. The method was this: Ryan would work out what franchises the syndicate wanted over what streets, and in what manner. Root would draft the franchises and attend to the Republican end, while Whitney handled the Democratic, or Tammany end through Richard Croker.

The Syndicate forced the stock of the Metropolitan Street Railway up to $253 a share and sold out on gullible speculators. **When Whitney, Widener and Elkins died, not a share of the securities of the companies which they had organized, exploited, and taken scores of millions from, were found in their estates.**

LOOTING THE GOOD OLD EDISON

H OW easy it is to make millions when you have a few corrupt political bosses to do your bidding and a lawyer like Root to advise you is shown by the way in which the Whitney-Ryan-Brady New York Gas, Electric Light, Heat & Power Company was organized and swallowed the good old Edison Company of New York City. The Edison Company had a franchise, great power houses, and was the pioneer in electric lighting. But its employees speedily encountered difficulties in repairing its

mains or extending its service and in getting City contracts. The Edison Company was finally forced to exchange its property for bonds of the Whitney-Ryan-Brady Company, which had had its wires put through many of the principal streets, *surreptitiously*, without any franchise whatever, by workmen who were supposed to be laying the underground cable system of the Metropolitan Street Railways.

Root also drew the proposition of the Metropolitan to build subways on the condition that the City give it a franchise in perpetuity, free of cost. **This was exposed by the Hearst papers and defeated.**

As Ryan's lawyer Root became counsel for the State Trust Company, controlled by Ryan. This was the banking institution through which the Metropolitan Syndicate conducted its fiscal operations.

One of the minority stockholders of the State Trust Company made formal charges to the Governor that illegal loans had been made to its directors, that the State Banking Law had been violated, and its assets misused, to the stockholders' loss. These charges were referred by the Governor to the Banking Superintendent, Frank D. Kilburn, who made an incomplete report, glossing matters over. The lawyer for the minority stockholders then made the public charge to the Governor that Superintendent Kilburn's report was not impartial because he was a friend of the notorious lobbyist, Lou Payn, who had borrowed $435,000 from the State Trust Company on security of uncertain value.

The Governor then appointed General Avery D. Andrews as special examiner. He **found that the State Trust Company had made questionable loans to the amount of $5,133,270.48.**

The largest of these loans was for $2,000,000 to Daniel E. Shea, the office manager of Ryan, the sole collateral being 20,000 shares each of Electrical Vehicle Preferred and New York Gas, Electric Light, Heat & Power Company stock, then worth much less than the loan.

LOANED $785,000 WITHOUT COLLATERAL!

ANOTHER loan was $785,000 to Anthony Brady, with no collateral. Another loan of $435,000 to William F. Sheehan, counsel for Anthony Brady, on Norwalk Street Railway and Gas Company stocks and bonds. The loan of $435,470 to Lou Payn, the notorious lobbyist, was secured in part by a certified check drawn by the Metropolitan Traction Company itself. **All of these loans were a gross violation of law.**

While Elihu Root was the legal adviser of Whitney and his associates, **the notorious Cortlandt Street franchise deal occurred.** This was a franchise granted by the Board of Aldermen without compensation for street car tracks from Broadway down to the Pennsylvania ferries, a distance of about one-quarter mile. **THE ROAD WAS NEVER BUILT,** Mr. Brady bought the franchise, which had cost nothing, from its owner, a lawyer, for about $10,000.

Messrs. Widener, Elkins, Whitney and Brady, in their dealings with politicians and others, had paid out very large sums of money for which they could not account on the books of the Metropolitan Street Railway so **they reimbursed themselves by adopting a resolution as directors of the Metropolitan Street Railway, to pay $3,000,000 for this franchise of Brady, which Brady bought for $10,000. The purchase was entered on the books of the Metropolitan as having cost $3,000,000! The money was divided between the five directors, including Elihu Root's client.**

This was another transaction which the Hearst papers later exposed. **To avoid suits for restitution,** threatened by legitimate stockholders of the Metropolitan Street Railway, **Elihu Root's client and his four associate directors paid back the money** into the treasury of the railroad.

So great was the power of these men that not one of them, nor any of their puppets in politics, or in the State Trust Company, or in the Metropolitan Street Railway, was ever prosecuted criminally.

BUT MORSE WAS SENT TO PRISON

A YEAR or two later Charles W. Morse, the Ice King, undertook some financial transactions which were considered hostile to another client of Mr. Root, the late J. P. Morgan. Morse tried to consolidate the Sound steamship lines in opposition to Morgan's New Haven Railroad. In one of his deals, Morse had his clerk, Leslie E. Whiting, put a dummy loan for $165,000 through the National Bank of North America, *a very much smaller transaction than*

Lawyer for Tweed who Looted New York!

Framed the Grab of the Edison Electric!

Told Whitney How to Take What He Wanted and Keep Out of Jail!

Figured in Five Billion Dollar Equitable Scandal!

Wrote a State Constitution That Was Overwhelmingly Repudiated by the People in a Referendum Vote of the State!

Now Heading the Organization Backed by Profiteering Plutocrats who are Denouncing Hearst!

the criminal acts exposed in the management of Mr. Ryan's State Trust Company when Root was its general counsel and director. CHARLES W. MORSE WAS SENTENCED TO FIFTEEN YEARS' IMPRISONMENT IN THE FEDERAL PENITENTIARY AT ATLANTA.

When the New York *World* asked Mr. Root if he had anything to say about the loan of $2,000,000 made to Daniel Shea, office boy for Ryan, Mr. Root replied: "There is nothing I care to say."

The report made to the Governor of New York by the State Banking Superintendent was that "the Shea loan was arranged for by Elihu Root as a director and member of the Executive Committee of the Trust Company and also as its counsel." If this official report was true, Mr. Root was liable to imprisonment in the penitentiary.

Root was also attorney of the Consolidated Gas Company and general counsel for the Metropolitan Street Railway Syndicate, and he fought the Franchise Tax Law of New York State, under which the State derives some income by taxing the franchises of public service corporations.

THE EQUITABLE LIFE SCANDAL

WHEN the corruption of the Equitable Life Insurance Company was exposed in 1905 and the stockholders sought to oust the young spendthrift, James H. Hyde, from the control of the company, Root appeared as Hyde's counsel. An Equitable policy holder appeared in court to protest against the payment of a fee of **a thousand dollars a day to Elihu Root as counsel for James H. Hyde.**

As a result of this fight, Hyde sold his stock to Mr. Root's other client, Thomas F. Ryan, who thus secured control of the **FIVE THOUSAND MILLION DOLLARS** of assets of the Equitable Life. The public scandal that ensued resulted in a change of management of all of the three great life insurance companies. The Equitable Life was sold to Morgan and the deed of trust was drawn by Root.

Since his retirement from the Senatorship, Root has taken little active part in politics except to draft the new Constitution of the State of New York, three years ago. **The people rejected this proposed Constitution by five hundred thousand majority, an unprecedented rebuke.**

Without Mr. Root's brains, his great ability and his acute legal knowledge, Ryan and Whitney would have been impossible. There would have been no traction merger, no such gas and electric light monopoly, no eight hundred million dollar capitalization of New York's public utilities; no defiance of the sovereignty of the State in taxing corporations.

THE BRAINS BEHIND THE BIG DEALS

FOR nearly thirty years Mr. Root has been the brains of the greatest Captains of High Finance who have enriched themselves by exploiting public franchises. He has carried out their schemes with extraordinary and unexampled zeal. The Hearst papers have exposed all and defeated many of these schemes with unexampled persistence and success.

The dearest ambition of Elihu Root's life was to end his career on the bench of the U. S. Supreme Court. He is a rich man. **But the exposure by the Hearst papers of his work as Ryan's and Morgan's lawyer made his appointment impossible.** Mr. Hearst's opposition to Root is purely upon public grounds. But Root's hatred of Hearst is purely personal because Hearst's exposure of Root defeated the great ambition of Root's life.

Elihu Root and Nicholas Murray Butler were incorporators of the Carnegie Corporation that gave $150,000 to the support of The National Security League last year. **One of the principal activities of the League speakers and workers was to attack Hearst.** The League is now under investigation of Congress for attacking the loyalty of more than 300 members of Congress.

Hearst and His Office Force Gave Over a Million Dollars to the Liberty Loan Drive

THE Hearst staffs in New York, Boston, Chicago, San Francisco. L s Angeles, and Atlanta, a total of 4,303 individuals, subscribed $474,750 to the Fourth Liberty Loan. **Hearst, himself, subscribed personally, the sum of $525,000 to make it AN EVEN MILLION for the Hearst outfit!**

This was in addition to a prior subscription which he made to the Mayor's Committee of Women, of which Mrs. William Randolph Hearst is chairman. The principal subscription was paid in New York, through the American Exchange National Bank, amounting to $701,350. After this was made, a last call came in from the Chicago district, and **Hearst came to the bat again, with an additional $100,000 subscription,** bringing the Hearst newspaper total, in that drive, up to $1,100,000.

Why The *Tribune* Fights Hearst

Owned By the Mills Estate, Which is Heavily Interested in New York Central and Southern Pacific, Both of Which Roads Hearst Halted in Big City Grabs!

Owners Related by Marriage to the Earl of Granard and also to the Equerry to the British King.

TO understand the psychology of *The New York Tribune's* attack on William Randolph Hearst, it is necessary to know something of the antecedents of *The Tribune*, and the class ties that now bind its ownership and management to English nobility on the one hand, and to large, predatory corporation interests on the other.

Once you grasp this great, outstanding fact, you get the truth of the whole situation.

Once you see clearly the powerful, vindictive motive behind this English newspaper's unparalleled campaign of falsification and vilification, you begin to understand the fight in all its angles, the reason for the assault, the object sought to be attained, and the anti-American interests that are to be served by a successful effort to misrepresent Hearst before the American public.

For the truth is that The New York Tribune is looked upon, to-day, as the recognized mouthpiece of Great Britain in America. It is more English than the London *Times,* and its editorials, at times, have been so vitriolic in their expression of anti-American hatred that even the **national leaders of America have had to brand its propaganda as dangerous** to the best interests of the United States.

These are hard things to say about any publication, rooted, as this one pretends to be, in the soil of free America, but we are really understating the case. The facts speak for themselves, as we shall presently show.

The *Tribune* has been able to pose before sincere patriots for a long time, because no one has taken the trouble to expose its un-American connections —to run down and disprove its false statements— and the Hearst papers, whose owner it has maligned throughout the land, have followed the foolish policy of ignoring it, in the belief that to reply or devote much space to the *Tribune's* attacks would merely be giving it much needed advertising and a hectic flush of intermittent circulation, which it very badly needed when it began the attack.*

OGDEN MILLS REID

Owner and Editor of The New York Tribune, who is a first cousin, by marriage, to the Earl of Granard, and a brother-in-law of the Hon. John Herbert Ward, Equerry to His Majesty King George. Through this latter connection, he is related to the first Earl of Dudley, whose second son may some day bring a coronet into the Reid family. The Reid fortune is buttressed by the millions that came down from old Darius Mills and represents holdings in 80 odd corporations, some twenty of which represent the big railroads of the United States, whose dividends will be vitally affected if Hearst's fight for government ownership wins!

WHY THE TRIBUNE ASSAILS HEARST

The reason for the *Tribune's* attack on Hearst is threefold:

FIRST—**The Tribune badly needed circulation.** It was a dying newspaper proposition, a drain upon the purse of the Mills Estate, which revived it, from time to time, with funds derived from a heavy interest in the big railroad corporations of America—notably the New York Central and the Southern Pacific. **An attack**

* [NOTE—The *Tribune* lost circulation steadily after it began its attacks on Hearst.]

35

on Hearst, on any grounds, would be a big selling sensation that would make circulation and draw much needed advertising The *Tribune* was desperate and it needed the money, even at the expense of wrecking a real American's good name and fame, and possibly exciting a nation to mob violence, in the hysterical period of a world war!

SECOND—The Mills and Reid families, who own the Tribune, are related by marriage to English nobility—one of the Mills girls having married the Earl of Granard, and Miss Reid having become the bride of the Hon. John Ward, Equerry to his Majesty the King of England. The *Tribune* ownership, soaked in the bias and prejudice of English nobility, transmitted through ties of wedlock, locked upon Hearst as a personal foe, because, in standing for " America First," he even went so far, at times, as to offend the ruling classes in Great Britain, who sought to have Uncle Sam play second fiddle to John Bull.

THIRD—The Mills Estate is heavily laden with hundreds of thousands of dollars' worth of stock in some of the great railroad corporations, which, within a few years, have attempted to seize valuable property rights in the heart

HON. JOHN H. WARD

Second son of the Earl of Dudley, one of the most aristocratic houses in England; Equerry to His Majesty, King George, and for whose children the King acted as godfather. Married Jean Reid, sister of Ogden Mills Reid (owner of The Tribune), and granddaughter of Darius O. Mills, whose millions, mostly in New York Central, Southern Pacific and International Paper Trust stock, have thus helped to maintain, in splendor, the traditions of the house of Dudley. The wedding was one of the most splendid ever witnessed at the Court of St. James. King Edward, Queen Alexandra, and princes of the blood attended. Whitelaw Reid's gift to the bride, his daughter, was a $500,-000 lodge, on which $100,000 additional was expended "to fit it up."

THE EARL OF GRANARD

Related to the Mills family, which owns The Tribune, by his marriage to Beatrice Mills, daughter of Ogden Mills, and granddaughter of Darius O. Mills, who left a half interest in $60,000,000 to her father. The other half of the Mills fortune went to Mrs. Whitelaw Reid, widow of the Ambassador to Great Britain. The Earl of Granard is Master of the King's Horse, and rides immediately behind the sovereign when the latter is on horseback, or else occupies the seat facing him in the royal carriage, on all public occasions. "His salary," says a London paper, " is $100,000 a year; but this, except in frugal hands, would not begin to keep up with the scale of magnificence in which the ... lives." The Countess of Granard is a first cousin ... n Mills Reid, the publisher of the New York

of New York—amounting in one case to many millions—and these grabs, notably the New York Central's attempt on the upper west side of Manhattan, and the Southern Pacific's notorious Rockaway Point deal, were both exposed and smashed by none other than Hearst and his newspapers. This kept a lot of honest graft out of the pockets of the Mills family.

With these few facts carefully set before you, the whole sordid drama of *The New York Tribune's* drive against Hearst, its effort to stir up race hatred, its cold-blooded game to get circulation, its atrocious campaign of lying, its propaganda, spread through pamphlets, containing misquoted, distorted and mutilated excerpts of editorials, becomes as plain as the noonday sun.

WHITELAW REID AND HORACE GREELEY

Let us look back a little at the history of *The New York Tribune* and see how some of the present actors managed to creep into its conning tower and take charge of the works. The *Tribune* was made famous by old Horace Greeley, than whom there was no one more beloved along the classic precincts of Park Row. Horace Greeley was a national figure, when, one day, a young man, who had made something of a name in journalism, came on to New York and established himself on the *Tribune*, under the direction of Greeley. **This young man was Whitelaw Reid, afterward owner of the Tribune, son-in-law of the fabulously rich Darius O. Mills, and Ambassador to England.**

Reid took hold, and, with the millions of the elder Mills, became a power in Park Row journalism; loomed up in the national councils of the Republican party, and was one day sent to the Court of St. James to represent America, as Ambassador to Great Britain.

IT was there, and at that time, that the seeds were sown, which have ripened into the perfect understanding that now exists between the ruling classes in England and the present management of *The New York Tribune*. Out of that Ambassadorial tenure of office in London, the introductions at Court, and the effort to shine in the snobbish society of nobility, grew **the friendship that led to the mingling of the Mills and Reid blood with aristocracy, and all the anti-American, prejudiced, British strain that characterizes the drift of the Tribune's editorial policy to-day.**

How high this swelling tide of pro-British feeling rose, in the *Tribune*, was evidenced by the vicious editorials that appeared soon after the armistice was signed and when President Wilson announced his stand on the celebrated "fourteen points" by which the world peace was to be decided.

THE TRIBUNE'S SLUR AT AMERICA!

THE *Tribune* was sarcastic in its reference to Wilson and the part played by America in winning the war. America's part was minimized and England's boldly blazoned forth. Excerpts from editorials in leading London newspapers were reprinted and a redhot propaganda was carried on, for days, in the *Tribune's* editorial columns, to show that Uncle Sam should take a back seat at the peace table and allow England to dominate the conference.

Here is what appeared on the editorial page of *The New York Tribune*, in the issue of November 22, 1918:

"It's none of our business—most things we horn in on, aren't—but the smugness of certain Americans who assume that we won this war and that now we are sending over a commission to rearrange the map of Europe, gives us a severe and unconquerable pain.

37

"Britain gave 650,000 lives to the cause. France gave more. We gave less than 20,000, and now certain folk cheep idiotically of the war that we won and of the peace that America will make for the world."

Could anything more dastardly than that have been uttered against the patriotism of a nation that gave of its men, its ships, its food, munitions and money, and whose people slaved and starved to rescue European civilization from the heel of Prussian autocracy?

All we have to do, is to picture Haig "with his back to the wall," down in the Ypres sector, calling madly for American help; the Prussian hordes within a few miles of the walls of Paris, and the whole fabric of the Allied defense about to crumble, when our boys made the dash at Chateau Thierry, and saved the day—to realize how false and hideous was this stand of *The Tribune*, that we were "presumptuous" in claiming that "we won the war."

What do the sincere, patriotic people who have been deceived by *The Tribune's* lying pamphlets about Hearst, think of this slap in the face, at America?

Could any distinctly insular British periodical, catering to a contemptible class of cads, in London, have said anything more bitter, and more calculated to rankle in the heart of an American, than this?

And, yet, this newspaper which utters such foul calumnies, against America, has been the instrument by which plutocracy's plunderers, all over the land, have vented their hatred against Hearst.

WHERE HEARST HAS OFFENDED

BUT, there is another, and just as important side, to *The Tribune's* attack on Hearst. The owner of the Hearst chain of newspapers has not only offended the British prejudice of *The Tribune* management by his fight for "America First"; the demand for the biggest navy in the world; the exaltation of the American soldiers, sailors and marines, for the part they played in winning the great world war—and his persistent fight for the recognition of Ireland, as a free and independent nation—**but Hearst has also mortally offended by his persistent attack upon plutocratic individuals with whom the Mills estate is closely allied in the management of great corporate institutions throughout the land.**

Take a look at what the elder Mills, the head of the line, left when he died about ten years ago, at the great age of 86. His wealth was estimated at close to $40,000,000, and this went to two children—Ogden Mills and Elizabeth Mills Reid, the widow of Whitelaw Reid, Ambassador to England, and directing head of the New York *Tribune.*

THE WEALTH OF DARIUS MILLS

DARIUS OGDEN MILLS was a storekeeper who sold goods to miners in California on speculation, taking a share of their gold findings for payment and interest. He was a kind of sutler following the great army of miners that struck it rich on the gold coast in 1849. He came on to New York in "the sixties," and began buying up real estate and putting the profit out in stock of all kinds of corporations. **When he died he was a director or part owner in no less than 48 railroad, oil, mining, iron, railway and lighting concerns, scattered all over America; 9 great banks in New York and California; and 28 industrial corporations**—few of them in less than six figures, and not a few showing his ownership of millions of dollars worth of controlling stock.

The schedule as revealed before the State Transfer Tax Appraiser, when the securities box was opened to assess the inheritance tax, **read like a national directory of corporations!**

New York Central led the list with 16,000 shares, valued at $1,996,000—**the corporation that tried, recently, to grab a $30,000,000 concession on the West side of Manhattan,** and in which *The Tribune* was so vitally interested. **This was the grab which the Hearst newspapers smashed.** Darius O. Mills also owned 15,878 shares of International Paper Company, preferred stock, and valued at $979,497, and likewise, bonds of the International Paper Company, amounting to $264,000, or **a total value of $1,243,497 in International Paper Trust alone.**

Now it is a fact of record that the New York Central was criminally prosecuted, convicted and fined by the government for giving rebates to the Sugar Trust, **upon evidence obtained and furnished by the Hearst newspapers. The International Paper Trust was also criminally prosecuted, last year, by the government under the Anti-Trust law.** In these two concerns themselves the Mills Estate are represented by an ownership of MORE THAN THREE MILLION DOLLARS!

Hearst's fights against plutocratic greed, as represented by Mills holdings, have hurt the pockets of the *Tribune's* owners, and hence, another powerful and deadly reason for the hate which the *Tribune* bears against Hearst!

(Continued on page 39.)

FREE WANT "ADS" FOR THE BOYS

HEARST started the boom to get "the boys"—the soldiers, sailors and marines who served with the colors in the great war—jobs, as soon as they got back. He gave up free to the men in the service the situation wanted "ad" columns of his great newspapers, to use as often as they wished to advertise for employment. The man's uniform, or, if in civilian clothes, his discharge papers, are the only passport needed to get the "ad" through free of charge. Thousands have availed themselves of this free service.

(Continued from preceding page.)

RAILROAD MONEY BEHIND TRIBUNE

LET us name a few other corporations, among the 80 odd, in which old Darius Mills was interested, when he died, and which interest has descended through the Mills and Reid families which now own and control The Tribune.

The list includes: Rock Island, $1,218,375; Atchison, Topeka and Santa Fe, $777,707; Portland Railway, $1,644,910; Peoples Gas Light & Coke, $1,227,117; Bunker Hill Mining, $1,230,600; Shredded Wheat, $1,140,150; **Standard Oil (600 shares), $394,600; Tide-water Oil (5,000 shares), $500,000;** Chicago, Rock Island and Pacific, $421,043; Coal and Coke Railway, $237,500; Erie, $86,000; Lake Shore, $81,068; Susquehanna and Western, $67,150; Pennsylvania Railroad (convertible bonds), $138,780; Seaboard Air Line (860 bonds), $614,900; **Southern Pacific (100 bonds), $105,625; Nassau Electric (83 bonds), $67,645;** American Steel, $56,925; **Kings County Electric (84 bonds), $94,920; International Paper Company (300 bonds), $264,000;** Atchison, preferred, $51,875; Chicago, and Northwestern (1,000 shares), $181,875; Chicago, Milwaukee and St. Paul (1,000 shares), $157,500; Northern Pacific (1,060 shares), $144,875; Rock Island, common (2,000 shares), $111,500; Seaboard Air Line, preferred (6,000 shares), $186,000; Seaboard Air Line, common (7,000 shares), $171,500; **Southern Pacific (2,454 shares), $333,437; Brooklyn Rapid Transit (8,106 shares), $646,453.**

Among the industrials of which Darius O. Mills died, possessed, and which have passed on down to The Tribune owners, are the following: American Steel Foundry, $140,334; Black Diamond Coal Mining, $112,065; Empire Coal and Coke, $118,776; Lackawanna Steel, $313,500; Buffalo Electric, $172,350; Commonwealth Edison of Chicago, $216,000; Duluth Edison, $85,000; Niagara Falls Power, $132,000; Northwestern Gas, $202,500; Pressed

Steel (1,000 shares), $106,500; Pullman Company (3,264 shares), $617,304; North Atlantic Steamship (605 shares), $206,032; Nevada Petroleum (56,250 shares), $196,875; Mesaba Steamship, $100,000; Alaska Mexican Gold Mining, $618,599.

In this list of railroads, oil, and industrials will be noted some of the corporations which have felt the weight of Hearst's editorial lash. We see Standard Oil, and its ally Tidewater Oil, represented in two allotments of stock totalling $894,600! Southern Pacific with 100 bonds, valued at $105,625 and 2,454 shares of stock at $333,437—a total of $439,062. It was a subsidiary concern of the Southern Pacific (the Rockaway Pacific Realty Company) that tried to jam the notorious Rockaway Point land deal, through the New York Legislature. The Hearst papers exposed a graft of $610,000 in that deal and killed the measure in the State Senate, of which body young Ogden L. Mills was at that time a member. The report of the Senate Committee which investigated the grab, denounced it as the worst attempt at profiteering under the guise of patriotism, that was ever attempted.

HOW THE FIGHT STARTED

IMMEDIATELY after the exposure of this deal by the Hearst newspapers, and following so closely upon the attack by Hearst, on the New York Central's attempt to monopolize the Hudson River front of Manhattan, the New York Central and its allied steamship lines, cancelled all advertising contracts, in the Hearst newspapers, from the Atlantic to the Pacific; the Southern Pacific cancelled all its advertising with Hearst, and The New York Tribune, owned by the Mills Estate, which is a heavy stockholder in these two corporations, BEGAN A SERIES OF FULL PAGE ARTICLES ATTACKING HEARST PERSONALLY.

That was the beginning of *The Tribune's* attack on Hearst. That's how this outrageous, malicious, scandalously lying propaganda was started! -

Hearst's great fight for government ownership of railroads was like a knife in the quivering body of the Mills Estate. It made every bone in *The Tribune* structure rattle. The money behind *The Tribune* comes from a score of big railroad properties—flowing easily from fat dividends, through the parasitic channels of capitalism. This is the tainted source from which the polluted breath of *Tribune* scandal issues.

It is because Hearst's fight for the people, to compel plutocracy to hand over to the nation, the great properties through which the people have been exploited, which have been employed to stock job and rig markets—has threatened the very existence of the Mills dividends, that *The Tribune's* foul attacks have been launched.

Every dollar that went into the moribund old *Tribune* to assail Hearst—because he dared to defy the alliance of corporation money behind the Mills family—represents an unearned increment, wrested from the public at one end and the product of labor at the other.

That is the kind of money that is fighting Hearst, and which, ever since he exposed the New York Central and Southern Pacific grabs, has never ceased to attack him through the columns of *The Tribune*.

(*Continued on page* 41.)

McADOO BRANDS THE TRIBUNE

HERE is what Secretary of the Treasury William G. McAdoo said of the *New York Tribune* at a time when that "loyal American" sheet was knocking the Liberty Loan. *The Tribune*, you know, is Hearst's worst defamer. Read what McAdoo says:

"I note that many of the newspapers express surprise that the German press claims that the two billion dollars Liberty Loan was a failure, in spite of the fact that it was greatly oversubscribed.

"THE GERMANS CAN SCARCELY BE BLAMED FOR MAKING SUCH CHARGES WHEN THE NEW YORK TRIBUNE PUBLISHED STATEMENTS, SHORTLY BEFORE SUBSCRIPTIONS CLOSED, THAT THE LOAN WAS HAVING "HARD SLEDDING" AND THAT IT WAS A FAILURE at that time in the sense that too much of its burden fell on the banks.

"I care nothing about the vicious Partisan attitude of the New York Tribune or its business manager, but I am concerned about the effect of their false and misleading statements. Such an extraordinary course by a leading New York newspaper and representative, calculated to injure the loan, is incomprehensible. THE ONLY EFFECT OF SUCH STATEMENTS, IF THAT BE OF SATISFACTION TO THEIR AUTHORS, IS THE COMFORT THEY HAVE GIVEN TO THE ENEMIES OF AMERICA."

THE NEW DANGEROUS PROPAGANDA

IT is said that, in addition to the money which rolls in fat dividends from a score of railroads throughout the United States—and from our own Brooklyn Rapid Transit Company, across the bridge, of which the Mills Estate owns $646,453 in stock— The Tribune is also supported mysteriously by the propagandist fund which has been launched in this country in the interest of British trade. If this be so, and we hope the rumor is unfounded, it may prove a serious matter at no distant date.

The day may soon come when American manufacturers will feel the crushing weight of discrimination in all parts of the world wherever British commerce secures an undue advantage; and should this condition be proved afterward to have been hastened by the policy of certain newspapers opposed to Hearst's motto of "America First," the said pro-British organs will surely feel the weight of American censure and condemnation.

The case of The Tribune, backed by all this corporation money, and brazenly supported by the lavish use of such funds, to further a wanton and audacious attack upon one who is regarded by millions as a champion of the people against the very agencies from which The Tribune draws its chief support, is perhaps one of the most glaring examples, in America, to-day of the manner in which the public press is being subsidized in the interest of corporate greed.

The facts speak plainly for themselves. Look at the array of corporations in which old Darius Mills' wealth is invested, and remember that this wealth, to-day, shapes the policy of The Tribune. Remember also that the schedule, as shown here, represented the values of ten years ago and recall the many fat financial melons that have been cut in that interval. Think of the manner in which the people have been exploited by some of these corporations, and remember that the blood money derived from such exploitation to-day gives life to the spread of plutocratic venom, expressed in hatred of one who has ceaselessly and tirelessly stood as the foe of greed and oppression as exemplified by these exploiting corporations.

If you feel the crushing effect of the high cost of living, it is because these great railroad plutocrats have taken their toll, from producer, farmer or manufacturer—as shipper, at one end, and the commission man and consumer at the other end. They have played with the stock, in one game after another, in the revels of Wall Street's many manipulations, and as in the case of the Brooklyn Rapid Transit, in which The Tribune's owners are heavily interested, they have left conditions which bred disaster and dismay in the midst of a long-suffering public.

The Tribune can't help but hate Hearst. It hates him like the "bad man" of the West hates a sheriff; like the wolf hates the herdsman—and it will continue to snarl and show its teeth so long as he continues to menace the game of its corporate masters. It hates him with all the hate that is born of plutocratic predatory lust; and it hates him with all the venom which newly acquired aristocratic pomp holds for the radical who seeks to thwart its un-American purpose.

WAR WORK OF THE TWO PAPERS COMPARED

AS the Mills Estate newspaper, the New York Tribune, was the "paper" that invented the attacks on Hearst, and his newspapers, because of their course in the war, it would seem to be proper to compare what the Hearst newspapers have done, with what the Mills Estate newspaper has done, to make the United States efficient in war, and to insure our victory over the enemy—the Imperial German government.

In the campaign to fill up vacancies in the Navy, the Marines, the regular army before and after the United States entered the war, the Tribune contributed, from April 1 to April 21, 1917, only 24 2-3 columns of space. The Hearst papers—The American and Evening Journal—on the other hand contributed this great total: 118 7-12 columns in the American, and 38 3-8 columns in the Evening Journal.

In the great effort to speed up Congress to give the President the Selective Draft Act, which he had asked, and which is now conceded to have been the most effective and logical means of securing an army that was, at the same time democratic and capable of dealing a speedy death blow to the enemy, the Tribune, from April 8 to April 30, 1917, inclusive, contributed 65 3-4 columns of space. In the same period the American (Hearst's morning paper) gave 119 1-4 columns of space, and the Evening Journal 55 1-8 columns.

During the twelve days the Selective Draft bill was pending in Congress The American printed a daily editorial and argument in its favor. The Mills Estate paper in these twelve days printed only four editorials, mildly advocating the bill, and not one editorial of condemnation of the Republicans who were opposing the bill.

To aid registration for the draft, after it became a law, mainly through the wide circulation of Hearst newspaper petitions, the Hearst papers contributed (American and Evening Journal) 289 columns, while The Tribune gave only 111 7-8 columns to the same campaign. In the second draft the figures were: Hearst papers, 77 columns; the Tribune, 33 1-4 columns.

RECORD IN THE RED CROSS CAMPAIGN

In the Red Cross Fund campaign the Hearst papers made a record of which they are proud. With cartoons, editorials, news matter and publicity of every sort the Hearst publications went to the bat and rolled up a total of 205 columns, while the *Tribune* contributed only 59 1-8 columns.

In the First Liberty Loan campaign to raise $3,000,000,000, as asked by Secretary McAdoo, the Hearst papers daily bombarded the public, and in the period from May 15 to June 15, 1917, inclusive, they printed 136 columns, while the *Tribune* published only 73 1-6 columns.

IN THE FOURTH LIBERTY LOAN DRIVE HEARST AND HIS STAFF GAVE OVER A MILLION DOLLARS! HOW MUCH DID THE TRIBUNE GIVE?

Seven thousand posters of Winsor McCay's great cartoon, "The Mailed Fist," showing Uncle Sam's mighty arm of dollars smashing the enemy, were used by the Government to spread American propaganda for the loan in 7,000 banks!

And this was the record all through the various campaigns, which the *Tribune* has attempted to misrepresent by the most infamous sort of lying propaganda.

If you meet someone who is quoting these falsehoods from the *Tribune*, pull out this pamphlet and read to him a few of these figures.

The only way to stop such lying is to go right back at it, with the facts!

How They Made Hearst Editorials Read Just the Other Way!

THE manner in which editorials from the New York American (Hearst's morning newspaper) have been misquoted and purposely garbled to give the impression that Hearst was opposed to the war, has been one of the amazing features of the campaign of calumny against the great and loyal American editor.

Let us give you a glaring example—every other sample can be proved false in just the same way. The files are open for inspection any day.

One of the quotations, taken in broken form, to deceive purposely, was that which appeared in the body of an editorial in the issue of April 27, 1917. Standing alone and with certain sections omitted (the omission being indicated in the Tribune by stars or dots), it reads one way; read in full it gives exactly the opposite meaning, the meaning the Tribune did not wish to convey.

It is an old trick—as old as the Sophists whom Socrates exposed in the ancient days of Athens.

And yet, for a long time, it fooled a great many really patriotic and sincere Americans who had never seen the whole editorial—never read it in its entirety.

The Tribune wanted to give the lying impression that Hearst was opposed to war. The garbled quotation would seem, faintly, to indicate that.

THE EDITORIAL, ITSELF, WHEN READ IN FULL, SHOWED THAT IT WAS A DEMAND TO MAKE READY FOR WAR—AN INSISTENT, CLAMOROUS CRY BY HEARST TO GET BUSY AND PREPARE FOR WAR.

It is called rhetorical legerdemain in journalism; it is called sophistry in logic; it is called misrepresentation in business—but, in plain everyday English, among regular folks, it is called "low down lying."

Here is what the Tribune charges:

"Once the United States declared war the Hearst papers opposed America's fighting a winning war against Germany. . . . They injected into the harmonies a piccolo diminuendo on the unwillingness of the people of the United States to enter the war.

"On April 27, 1917, the New York American said: 'Gentlemen of the Congress of the United States, you have put us into war. . . . If the folks at home did not want to go to war, it was your duty to think of that BEFORE YOU DECLARED WAR.'"

This sounds terrible when you read this, and this alone. That's what many good people thought—and they based their sincere denunciation of Hearst, on stuff like this, without ever going back to see if it were true.

This would give the impression that "the folks at home"—referred to the American people—and that they did not want war. Hearst had merely taken up a "catch phrase" of

(Continued on page 44.)

"CONGRESS' DUTY TO GIVE MEANS FOR VICTORY;"
"VOLUNTEER FORCE LEAST EFFECTIVE PLAN"

Washington, April 27.—The Washington Post publishes the following on its first page to-day:—

AN OPEN LETTER
By William Randolph Hearst.

To the Hon. Champ Clark:

Dear Friend and Respected Sir—You know that I am a devoted admirer and supporter of yours and that every word in this utterance is written in sincerity and friendship.

Indeed, I speak only out of loyalty to my friends and to my country and in the earnest hope that I may be able to say something which will help to persuade you and my other friends and former associates in Congress to take the course in regard to universal service which will be most beneficial to yourselves as representatives of the people and to the dear country which we all love and seek to serve.

Let me begin by saying that SERVICE is not SERVITUDE and the two words are NOT to be confounded in the minds of the intelligent people of the United States.

There is the widest possible difference between PATRIOTIC SERVICE and PENAL SERVITUDE, and that difference is clearly defined in the minds and hearts of all good citizens.

A CONSCRIPT is not a CONVICT and the only discredit attached to the conscript in times past was due to the fact that he was in some instances a coward compelled by force to do his duty to his country after the brave men had voluntarily offered to render their patriotic service.

Had all men been requisitioned by the Government at once there would have been no distinction between strong and weak, between brave and timid, and consequently no discredit upon PATRIOTIC SERVICE under governmental levy.

Universal service as now proposed is merely the [EDUCATION] of the young men of the [ ] important and patriotic of all public [ ] the nation's defense.

There is no more discredit or di[ ] of compulsory education than there [ ] COMPULSORY EDUCATION. In [ ] honor and a greater glory and a [ ] higher opportunity in this form of ed[ ] form of education that our great co[ ] tions require or afford.

The object of this education—th[ ] flies and our fellows, the safeguardin[ ] tutions and standards, the perpetuat[ ] ciples and liberties, the defense of [ ] noblest object and obligation of our [ ]

Moreover, a course in military [ ] men is of much an advantage to them [ ] nation.

A course in military training is, first, [ ] training, and such a course is of prime imp[ ] ing and developing the PHYSICAL EXC[ ] people and of our race.

A course in military training is, second, [ ] a course in discipline, and such a course is most important in developing the MORAL CALIBRE AND CHARACTER of our youth and our people.

A course in military training is, third, a course in system and organization and efficiency; and what our nation and our people most need for the adequate development of the immense resources in our country and within ourselves is UNIVERSAL TRAINING IN SYSTEM, ORGANIZATION AND EFFICIENCY.

A course in military training for our young men, therefore, will make better private citizens of our people, fitting them better to discharge their private duties as well as preparing them adequately and effectively to discharge their highest public functions.

A course in military training, then, would be of the highest benefit to the individual and to the nation, even if there were never to be another war. But we all know now that there will be wars until men are more civilized, and that it would be criminal folly for our nation not to prepare to protect ourselves against wars which are sure to occur and some of which are sure to be directed against us.

No nation has ever hoped more earnestly for peace and striven more ardently to stay out of war than has our nation during the past five years. Yet during the greater part of that time we have been constantly baited and bullied, insulted and attacked, injured and actually invaded, until finally we were forced into war in defense of our honor, our rights, our liberties and our lives.

The outrages committed by so-called barbarous Mexico to the south of us were almost equaled by alleged civilized nations of Europe, until war became inevitable and unavoidable in spite of our high humanitarian ideals and our utmost pacific endeavors.

Since war, then, may be so evidently forced upon us at any time, and since the present war may be at any time so extended, (according to recent diplomatic declarations) as to menace our national integrity and independence, the problem we confront and must confront is how most effectively to meet and defeat warlike offensives launched against us.

It is a primary principle of warfare that success is achieved by concentrating the utmost force at critical points in the promptest manner.

Now, the volunteer system does NOT provide the most possible force, NOR does it provide the force in the promptest possible time. On the contrary it probably provides the smallest possible force in the longest possible time, and is,

therefore, THE LEAST [ ] OF MILITARY [ ] great war METHODS. [ ] is left for the adequate [ ] of a republic by duly democratic and properly effective methods only UNIVERSAL SERVICE.

Gentlemen of the Congress of the United States, YOU HAVE PUT US INTO WAR, and it is your duty now to give the sufficient and efficient MEANS OF MAKING WAR.

If the "folks at home" did not want to go to war, it was your duty to think of that BEFORE YOU DECLARED WAR.

It is in no way right or reasonable or wise or patriotic for you to project the nation into war and then, out of unfounded fear for your own future, deny the nation the method best qualified and calculated to make VICTORIOUS WAR.

If you are unwilling to run the small risk of losing your seats in Congress in the moment of [ ] right had you to call upon others [ ] thers to risk [ ]

[ ] and suffering of this great war, which [ ] nearer to our shores and our doors?

Mr. Speaker and dear friend, my father and mother came from Missouri, as you do, and I think that through family association I know something of the sentiment of the people of Missouri. I confidently venture the assertion that in no spot in all this broad land of ours are the people more proud of their country, more patriotically devoted to its best interests, more willing to sacrifice themselves and their personal comfort and convenience to the general welfare of theirs and our great and beloved United States of America.

I venture the assured and emphatic assertion that the only risk a Congressman from Missouri or from any other State runs of displeasing the "folks at home" is by hesitating in this time of national crisis to do his patriotic duty fully and unselfishly—is by failing to give the "folks at home" and the nation at large the protection through universal service which the whole country requires and desires.

WILLIAM RANDOLPH HEARST.

43

(*Continued from page* 42.)

a Congressman who was complaining that his constituency was opposed to the Selective Draft act. This man said—"the folks at home did not approve of conscription." Hearst was merely going back at him. It was no time to be thinking of that now. War was declared and we were in it—and had to win it.

The congressman whom Hearst was twitting was afraid he might lose his seat in the House if he displeased "the folks at home." Here is what Hearst said, AND WHAT THE TRIBUNE WAS CAREFUL TO CONCEAL:

"I venture the assured and emphatic assertion that the only risk a Congressman from Missouri or from any other State runs of displeasing the 'folks at home' is by hesitating in this time of national crisis to do his patriotic duty fully and unselfishly—is by failing to give the 'folks at home' and the nation at large the protection through universal service which the whole country requires and desires."

Hearst, in fact, was in Washington at the time, doing his best to win Congress over to the speedy passage of the Selective Act.

By omitting in the fraudulent quotation the words here set in caps, a New York Tribune quotation distorter—as will be seen—changed the entire meaning of the quotation and falsified the purpose of the editorial: "You have put us into war, AND IT IS YOUR DUTY NOW TO GIVE THE SUFFI-CIENT AND EFFICIENT MEANS OF MAKING WAR."

The amazing fraudulent purpose of this misquotation becomes apparent when one reads the whole editorial. It is one of the strongest pleas Hearst ever made to help in winning the war.

All this time, at the very moment when Hearst was supposed, according to this mis-quotation, to be opposing war, his papers were making earnest daily appeals to have the selective law passed.

Those daily appeals, backed up by more than 2,000,000 individual signed peti-tions from Hearst newspaper readers, had greater effect in crystallizing public opinion in favor of this law—according to Representative Kahn, the sponsor for the bill in Washington—than any other agency outside Washington.

Would you believe that such a monstrous falsehood could be so boldly circulated and taken seriously by patriotic bodies throughout the country without any verification, and be accepted as gospel by thousands of honest, true-hearted American folk?

And yet that's the underhanded way this whole anti-Hearst campaign has been carried on.

Those Who Sell Their Pens

The Paid Propagandists assailing Hearst are controlled for the most part, by the profiteers, who have bled the public, during the war.

IN Babylon, high Babylon,
   What gear is bought and sold?
All merchandise beneath the sun
   That bartered is for gold;
Amber and oils from far beyond
   The desert and the fen,
And wines whereof our throats are fond—
   Yea! and the souls of men!

In Babylon, dark Babylon,
   Who take the wage of shame?
The scribe and singer, one by one,
   That toil for gold and fame.
They grovel to their master's mood;
   The blood upon the pen
Assigns their souls to servitude—
   Yea! and the souls of men!

—From George Stirling's powerful poem, "In the Market Place."

"Hell and Destruction Are Never Full; So the Eyes of Men Are Never Satisfied."—PROVERBS XXVII. 20.

TRUTH. JUSTICE **New York American Editorial Page** PUBLIC SERVICE

Thursday, May 24, 1917

The Mailed Fist of Uncle Sam Must Be Armed with American Dollars

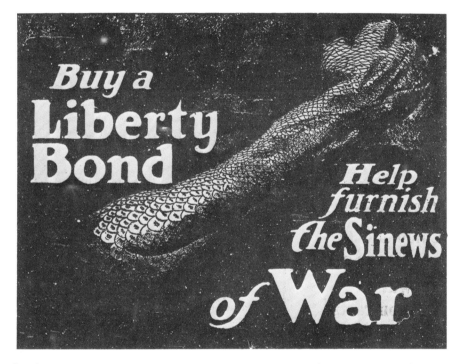

Buy a **Liberty Bond**

Help furnish the Sinews of War

THE Liberty Loan Committee had 7000 posters of this great cartoon struck off to send to every Federal Bank in the United States, to aid in the local campaigns for the Loan drive. Ask these banks what they thought of it!

PERSECUTION

"The history of persecution is a history of endeavors to cheat nature. * * * Every lash inflicted is a tongue of fame; every prison a more illustrious abode; every burned book or house enlightens the world; every suppressed or expunged word reverberates through the earth from side to side. The minds of men are at last aroused; reason looks out and justifies her own and malice finds all her work in vain. It is the whipper who is whipped, and the tyrant who is undone."

—*Ralph Waldo Emerson's Essay on "Compensation."*

SYNOPSIS OF SOME OF THE BIG FIGHTS
HEARST HAS WAGED FOR THE PEOPLE

Gas Trust!

Ice Trust!

Beef Trust!

Coal Trust!

Traction Trust!

N. Y. Cen. Grab!

Rockaway Steal!

Standard Oil!

Brooklyn Rotten Transit!

Food Profiteers!

Commandeer Munitions!

Subway Contracts!

Government Ownership!

And many other Battles to Protect the Public in its Rights Against Corporate Greed!

HEARST has often offended the "powers that prey" by his many fights for the people. Hearst, in the eyes of the criminal rich, is a menace, and hence must be destroyed, like Carthage.

He has plucked the mask from the face of invisible government, and revealed the power behind the throne.

It was he who procured photographic copies of the Standard Oil letters, purchasing United States Senators at $25,000 a head. He read and published these all over the country in 1908!

He compelled the Coal Trust to dissolve its illegal combination—by which coal carrying roads owned the coal in the mines from which they hauled.

He fought the Beef Trust, Ice Trust, and started the investigation of the Gas Trust which brought about 80-cent gas in Greater New York.

He exposed the gigantic robbery in the dual Subway contracts and saved the city $11,000,000! This was a direct assault on the Morgan banking firm, which was done out of preferential dividends.

Hearst has hammered, all down the years, at every capitalistic head that rose to rob.

His fight for government ownership—including railroads, telephones, telegraphs and coal mines—has brought down upon him a storm the like of which no individual ever encountered. This doctrine goes to the very root of all the big graft in the United States. It interferes with the easy money of every blood-sucking parasite in every profiteering concern in the country.

Hearst, pounding this doctrine out to 15,000,000 readers in the United States, every day, has struck terror into the hearts of the whole plunderbund. It shakes the very citadel of plutocracy. The latter has called to its army of retainers and the result is this amazing war on Hearst.

His fight is yours and mine!

Shall we allow them to destroy him?

Wherever You Find the FOES OF HEARST There You'll Find the OPPRESSORS of the PEOPLE

What Hearst Says About the Concentration of Big Money in the Hands of Exploiters!

THESE great Foundations (the Carnegie and Rockefeller Foundations) are the foes of the public, the enemies of popular rights, the persistent and powerful agents of the privileged classes in maintaining their unjust privileges and in slandering the public servants who believe in equal rights and equal opportunities and who oppose special privileges.

"An estimate by a leading financier, places the income of the Rockefeller fortune at twelve million dollars a month. * * * The conditions which permit the accumulation of these vast fortunes, if continued, eventually involve the republic in ruin."

"But most dangerous of all are these great political foundations, created out of this hoard of plunder for the purpose of protecting the plunder and the plunderers and of perpetuating the conditions of monopoly and political favoritism which make the accumulation of such immense and illegitimate fortunes possible.

"Congress should proceed to protect not only its own members but the country from this dangerous misapplication of the power of predatory wealth.

"The Rockefeller Foundation is probably the most menacing influence in the public life of America. The sniveling hypocrisy that stands with a Bible in one hand and a bribe in the other, has been thoroughly exposed heretofore in the articles of Ida Tarbell in *McClure's Magazine* and in the widely published Standard Oil Letters.

"END THIS DOLLAR DESPOTISM"—

"Congress should end this dollar despotism, this tyranny of wealth, this arrogant autocracy of privilege."

As a means to end this "autocracy of privilege," Hearst recommends that Congress should immediately have the nation take over these foundations and all similarly menacing bodies.

To prevent further accumulations of increasing fortunes he suggests "an income tax of at least 90 per cent. on all personal income of any individual in excess of five million dollars a year" and a tax "of 95 per cent. on all personal income of any individual in excess of ten million dollars a year."

As a clincher to prevent the growth of dangerous fortunes he proposes "a permanent inheritance tax of 50 per cent. for all fortunes over $20,000,000, or some such set sum, the inheritance tax decreasing on smaller fortunes, until it disappears entirely on modest inheritances."

To make this kind of an inheritance tax effective, he says "it ought not be possible for the possessor of a large fortune to convey during his lifetime to anyone, who could figure as an heir under his will, any sum of money without paying the inheritance tax."

BOLDLY ADVISES CONFISCATION—

He would punish WITH CONFISCATION "any attempt to evade the inheritance tax law."

"The idea," says Hearst, "frequently expressed by great writers on democracy, that monarchies are destroyed by poverty and republics by wealth, is unquestionably a true idea; and honest citizens and honorable public officials who desire to retain for the people the advantage of republican institutions and democratic equality and opportunity, should take care that wealth does not and cannot accumulate to the point where it will be a danger to the country."

A Hand-Book of Red Hot Facts

This Booklet comprises, in a handy compass, facts about the profiteers, the great fortunes they have reaped in the late war, and other features which have developed out of this fight on Hearst, which you will find of great help in explaining the truth to your friends: Carry It with you and back up your argument with facts!

The Committee of Relatives of American Soldiers, Sailors and Marines of Greater New York was organized by men who have known Hearst for years, and who feel deeply grateful for the splendid fight he is making in behalf of the men who have served the colors, and now find themselves in need of a champion, as they return to seek the jobs they left, when they rushed to defend the flag. They selected Edward T. O'Loughlin, formerly Registrar of Brooklyn, whose relatives have served in the war, to prepare this pamphlet in their name.

Show This Book to Your Neighbor

Additional copies of this booklet may be obtained by mailing ten cents in stamps to The O'Loughlin Company, Inc., Temple Bar Building, 44 Court Street, Brooklyn. Organize a bundle committee in your neighborhood and spread the good work. Special rates to clubs and newsdealers.

There is a reason for every knock on Hearst. If you are fair-minded after reading this booklet, you will confess the propaganda launched against this great American is one of the most malicious and unjust ever inaugurated to defame a just man.

Hearst's Fight Is Yours and Mine